Two Story Homes

Design 152713

1,830 Sq. Ft. - First Floor
1,056 Sq. Ft. - Second Floor
41,370 Cu. Ft.

● Here is a picture of Early Colonial charm that is certain to impress even the most casual passer-by. The appeal of the Gambrel roof contrasts pleasingly with the delightfully detailed gabled-roof garage. The interior is no less outstanding with all that formal and informal living potential. The kitchen-nook-family room area is wonderfully spacious. Don't miss the service entrance.

1

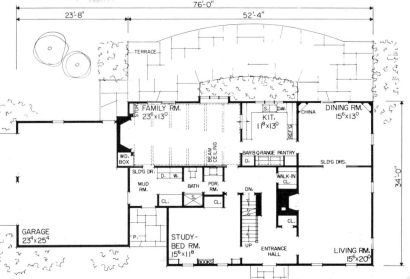

Design 151900

1,672 Sq. Ft. - First Floor
1,287 Sq. Ft. - Second Floor
42,050 Cu. Ft.

● The history of the Colonial Salt Box goes back some 200 years. This unusually authentic adaptation captures all the warmth and charm of the early days both inside as well as outside. To reflect today's living patterns, an updating of the floor plan was inevitable. The result is a room arrangement which will serve the active family wonderfully. Study the interior carefully. It is outstanding for the large, active family of today.

Design 152399

1,301 Sq. Ft. - First Floor
839 Sq. Ft. - Second Floor
34,743 Cu. Ft.

● A typical New England Salt Box with authentic front door detailing. The formal entrance hall features open, curved staircase. There are two large living areas, an excellent kitchen/nook layout and a downstairs bedroom.

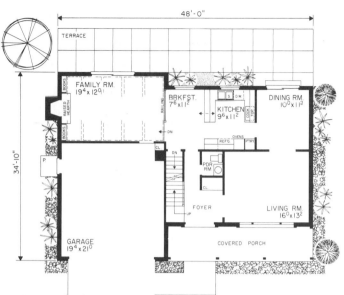

OPTIONAL 3 BEDROOM PLAN

Design 151956 990 Sq. Ft. - First Floor
728 Sq. Ft. - Second Floor; 23,703 Cu. Ft.

Design 152211

1,214 Sq. Ft. - First Floor
1,146 Sq. Ft. - Second Floor
32,752 Cu. Ft.

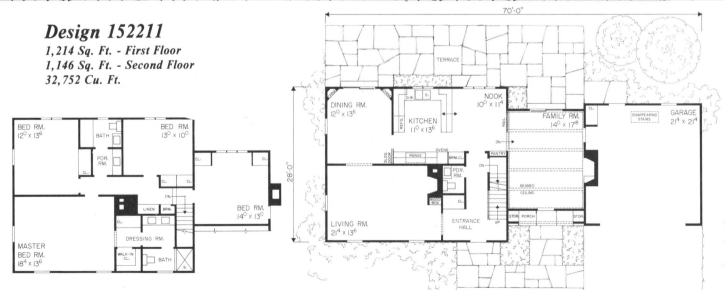

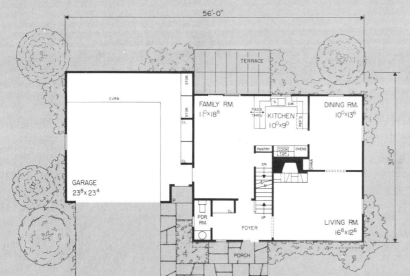

Design 151719

864 Sq. Ft. - First Floor
896 Sq. Ft. - Second Floor
26,024 Cu. Ft.

Design 152101

1,338 Sq. Ft. - First Floor
1,144 Sq. Ft. - Second Floor
39,617 Cu. Ft.

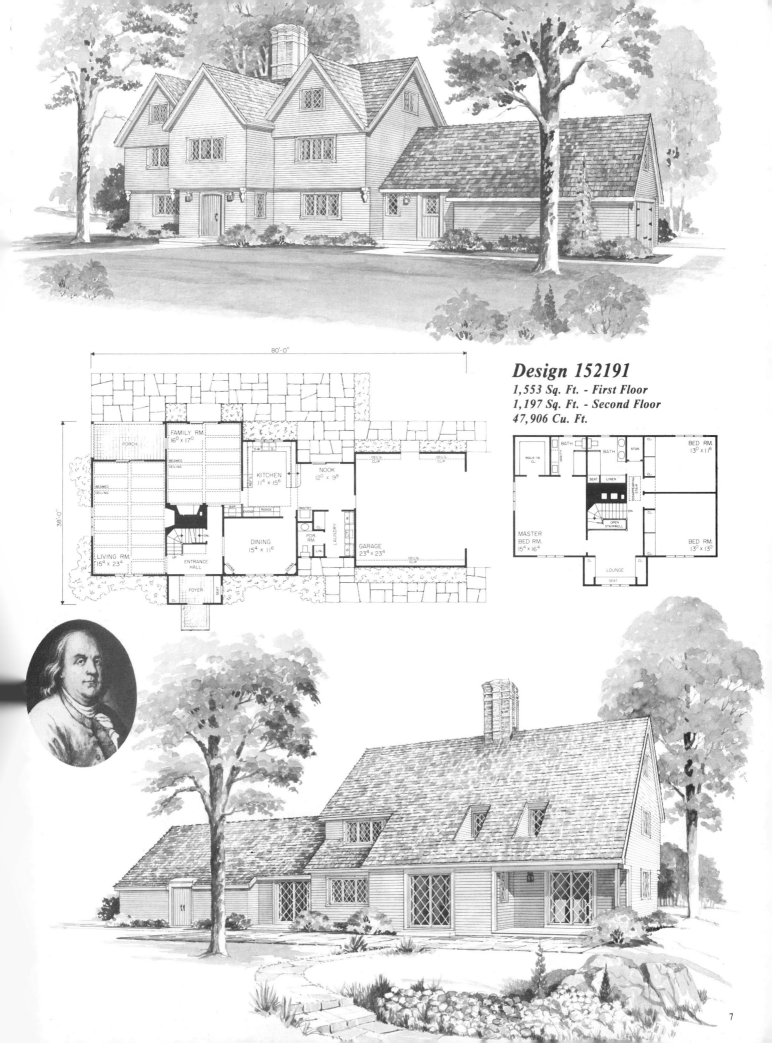

Design 152191

1,553 Sq. Ft. - First Floor
1,197 Sq. Ft. - Second Floor
47,906 Cu. Ft.

First Floor:

- PORCH
- FAMILY RM. 16⁰ x 17⁰
- BEAMED CEILING
- KITCHEN 11⁴ x 15⁶
- NOOK 12⁰ x 9⁸
- CEIL'G CLIP
- BEAMED CEILING
- LIVING RM. 15⁴ x 23⁴
- ENTRANCE HALL
- UP
- DINING 15⁴ x 11⁶
- BAR - OVENS - RANGE
- PANTRY
- PDR. RM.
- LIN
- LAUNDRY
- GARAGE 23⁴ x 23⁴
- CEIL'G CLIP
- FOYER
- CL.
- SEAT

80'-0"
38'-0"

Second Floor:

- WALK-IN CL.
- BATH
- BATH
- STOR.
- BED RM. 13⁰ x 11⁶
- SEAT
- LINEN
- DISAPPEARING STAIR
- OPEN STAIRWELL
- DN.
- MASTER BED RM. 15⁴ x 16⁴
- BED RM. 13⁰ x 13⁰
- LOUNGE
- SEAT

7

Design 152188

1,440 Sq. Ft. - First Floor
1,280 Sq. Ft. - Second Floor
40,924 Cu. Ft.

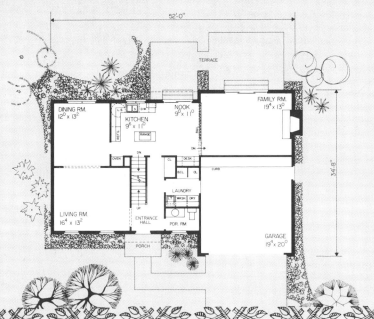

Design 152733

1,177 Sq. Ft. - First Floor
1,003 Sq. Ft. - Second Floor
32,040 Cu. Ft.

First floor labels: DINING RM. 12⁰ x 13², KITCHEN 9⁶ x 11⁰, NOOK 9⁰ x 11⁰, FAMILY RM. 19⁴ x 13⁰, RANGE, LS, REF'G, OVEN, DN, CL, DESK, BCL, CL, CURB, DN, UP, LAUNDRY, LT, WASH, DRY, LIVING RM. 16⁴ x 13², ENTRANCE HALL, PDR. RM., GARAGE 19⁴ x 20⁰, PORCH, TERRACE

52'-0", 34'-8"

Second floor labels: MASTER BED RM. 11⁰ x 15⁴, BED RM. 11⁰ x 9⁴, CL, BATH, DN, LINEN, BATH, CL, CL, LINEN, BOOKS, DESK, BED RM. 14⁴ x 12⁸, BED RM. 11⁰ x 12⁸

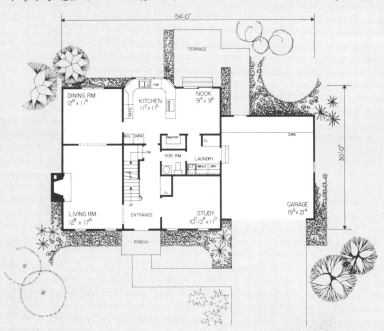

Design 152731

1,039 Sq. Ft. - First Floor
973 Sq. Ft. - Second Floor
29,740 Cu. Ft.

First floor labels: DINING RM. 12⁸ x 11⁶, KITCHEN 11⁰ x 11⁶, NOOK 9⁴ x 9⁶, DW, REF'G, RANGE, BCL, OVEN, PANTRY, CL, DN, PDR. RM., LAUNDRY, LT, WASH, DRY, CURB, CL, UP, LIVING RM. 12⁸ x 17⁶, ENTRANCE, STUDY 10² 12⁴ x 11⁰, GARAGE 19⁸ x 21⁴, PORCH, TERRACE

54'-0", 30'-0"

Second floor labels: ROOF, BED RM. 17⁰ x 11⁶, BATH, S, WALK IN CLOSET, ROOF, DN, LINEN, BATH, CL, MASTER BED RM. 12⁸ x 17⁶, RAILING, BED RM. 12⁴ x 12²

9

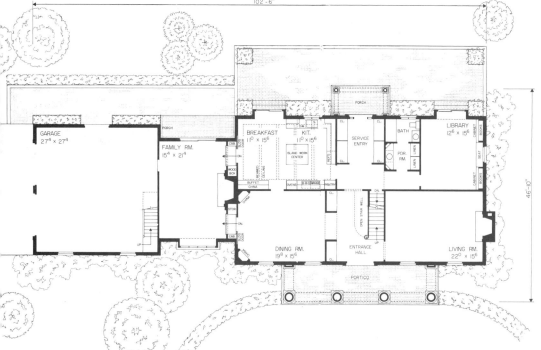

Design 152230

2,288 Sq. Ft. - First Floor
1,863 Sq. Ft. - Second Floor
79,736 Cu. Ft.

● The gracefulness and appeal of this southern adaptation will be everlasting. The imposing two-story portico is truly dramatic. Notice the authentic detailing of the tapered Doric columns, the balustraded roof deck, the denticulated cornice, the front entrance, and the shuttered windows. The architecture of the rear is no less appealing. The spacious, formal front entrance hall provides a fitting introduction to the scale and elegance of the interior. The openness of the stairwell provides a view of the curving balusters above.

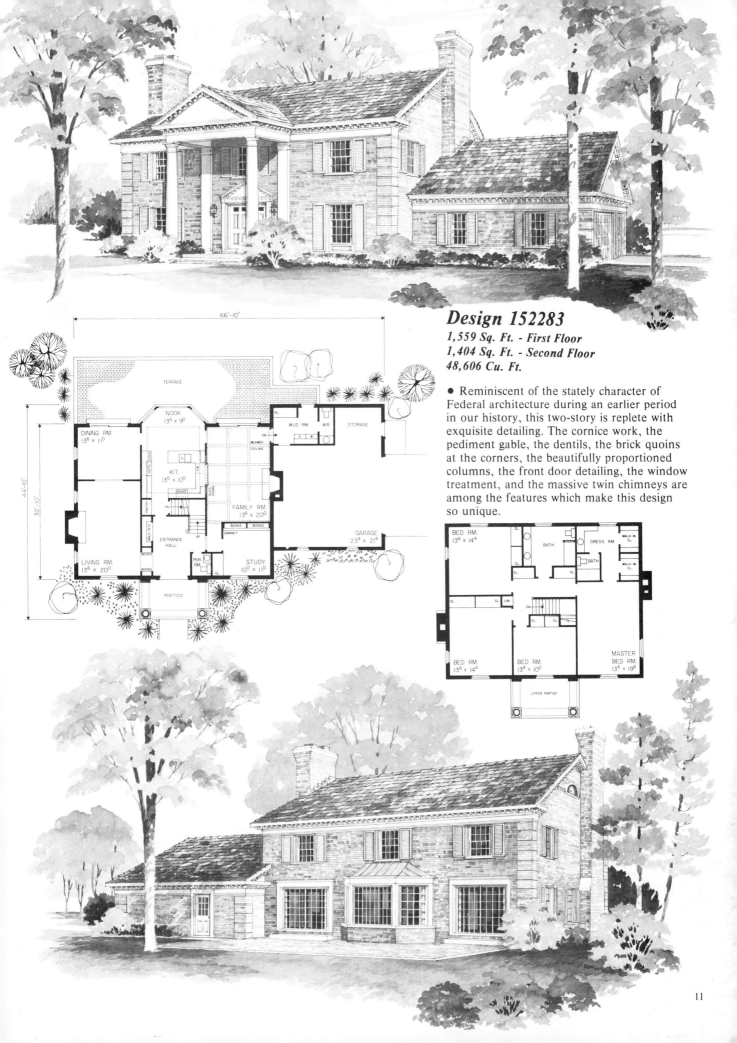

Design 152283

1,559 Sq. Ft. - First Floor
1,404 Sq. Ft. - Second Floor
48,606 Cu. Ft.

● Reminiscent of the stately character of Federal architecture during an earlier period in our history, this two-story is replete with exquisite detailing. The cornice work, the pediment gable, the dentils, the brick quoins at the corners, the beautifully proportioned columns, the front door detailing, the window treatment, and the massive twin chimneys are among the features which make this design so unique.

First Floor Plan labels:

66'-10"
44'-10"
32'-10"

TERRACE
NOOK 13⁶ x 9⁰
DINING RM. 13⁶ x 11⁰
MUD RM.
W.R.
STORAGE
BEAMED CEILING
KIT. 13⁶ x 10⁰
RANGE
FAMILY RM. 13⁶ x 20⁰
BOOKS
CABINET
GARAGE 23⁴ x 21⁴
ENTRANCE HALL
UP
LIVING RM. 13⁶ x 20⁰
PDR. RM.
STUDY 10⁰ x 11⁰
WALK-IN CL.
PORTICO

Second Floor Plan labels:

BED RM. 13⁶ x 14⁴
BATH
DRESS. RM.
WALK-IN CL.
BATH
WALK-IN CL.
CL.
LIN.
DN
BED RM. 13⁶ x 14⁴
BED RM. 13⁸ x 10⁰
MASTER BED RM. 13⁶ x 19⁶
UPPER PORTICO

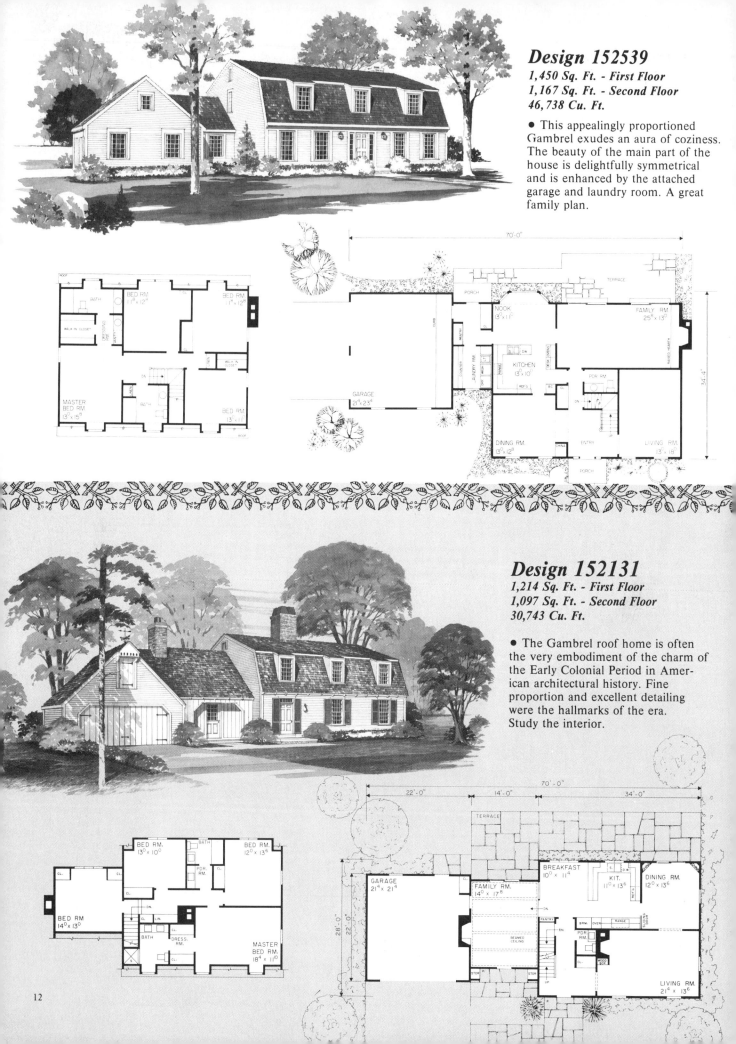

Design 152539

1,450 Sq. Ft. - First Floor
1,167 Sq. Ft. - Second Floor
46,738 Cu. Ft.

● This appealingly proportioned Gambrel exudes an aura of coziness. The beauty of the main part of the house is delightfully symmetrical and is enhanced by the attached garage and laundry room. A great family plan.

Design 152131

1,214 Sq. Ft. - First Floor
1,097 Sq. Ft. - Second Floor
30,743 Cu. Ft.

● The Gambrel roof home is often the very embodiment of the charm of the Early Colonial Period in American architectural history. Fine proportion and excellent detailing were the hallmarks of the era. Study the interior.

Design 151986

896 Sq. Ft. - First Floor
1,148 Sq. Ft. - Second Floor
28,840 Cu. Ft.

● This Gambrel roof design spells charm wherever it may be situated - far out in the country, or on a busy thoroughfare. Compact and economical to build, it will be easy on the budget. There's a full basement, too.

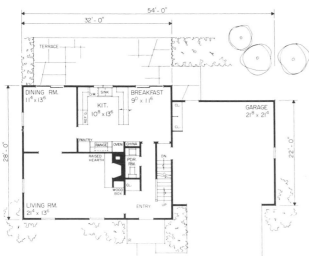

Design 152617

1,223 Sq. Ft. - First Floor
1,018 Sq. Ft. - Second Floor
30,784 Cu. Ft.

● Another Gambrel roof version just loaded with charm. Notice the delightful symmetry of the window treatment. Inside, the large family will enjoy all the features that assure convenient living. The end-living room will have excellent privacy.

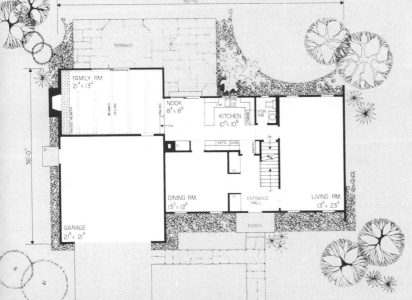

13

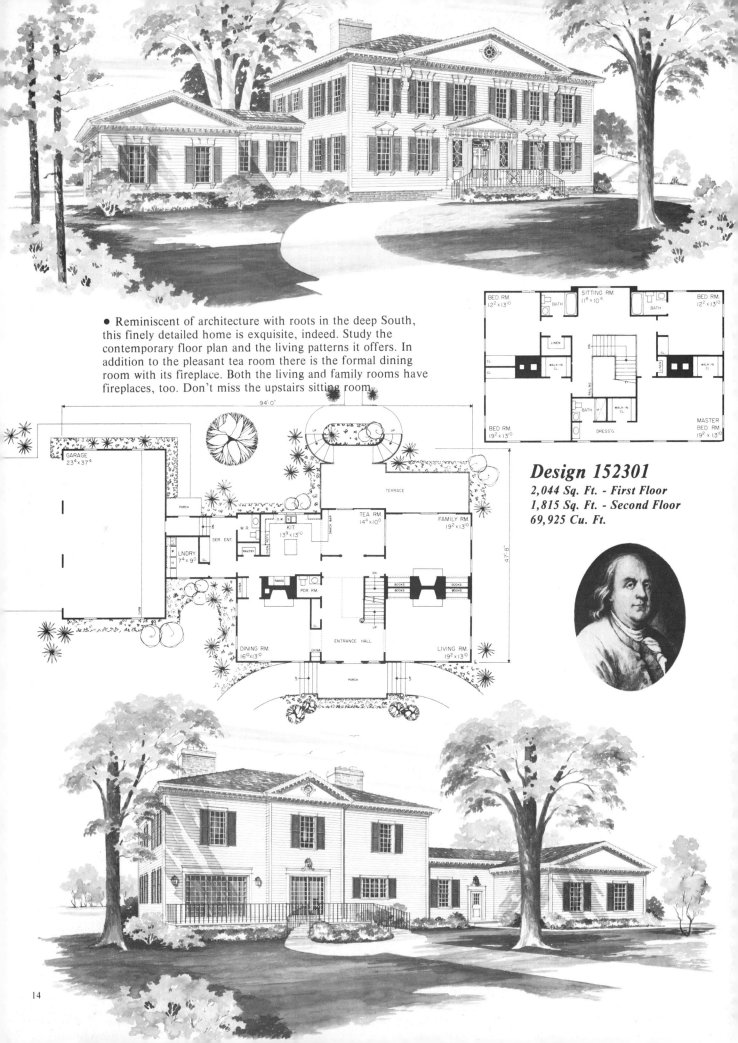

• Reminiscent of architecture with roots in the deep South, this finely detailed home is exquisite, indeed. Study the contemporary floor plan and the living patterns it offers. In addition to the pleasant tea room there is the formal dining room with its fireplace. Both the living and family rooms have fireplaces, too. Don't miss the upstairs sitting room.

Design 152301

2,044 Sq. Ft. - First Floor
1,815 Sq. Ft. - Second Floor
69,925 Cu. Ft.

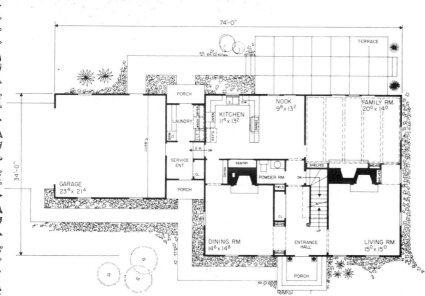

• Here is a New England Georgian adaptation with an elevated doorway highlighted by pilasters and a pediment which gives way to a second-story Palladian window, capped in turn by a pediment projecting from the hipped roof. The interior is decidedly up-to-date with even an upstairs lounge.

74'-0"

34'-0"

TERRACE

PORCH

NOOK
9⁸ x 13²

FAMILY RM.
20⁰ x 14⁰

LAUNDRY

KITCHEN
11⁴ x 13²

GARAGE
23⁴ x 21⁴

SERVICE ENT.

PANTRY

POWDER RM.

DINING RM.
14⁶ x 14⁸

ENTRANCE HALL

LIVING RM.
15⁰ x 15⁰

PORCH

BED RM.
15⁰ x 10⁰

BATH

VANITY

BED RM.
14⁰ x 15⁰

BATH

DRESSING RM.

LINEN

BED RM.
15⁰ x 12⁸

LOUNGE
10⁸ x 7⁸

MASTER BED RM.
15⁰ x 15⁰

Design 152639 *1,556 Sq. Ft. - First Floor; 1,428 Sq. Ft. - Second Floor; 46,115 Cu. Ft.*

Design 152538

1,503 Sq. Ft. - First Floor
1,095 Sq. Ft. - Second Floor
44,321 Cu. Ft.

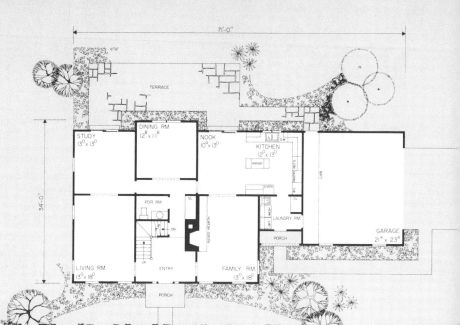

Design 152253

1,503 Sq. Ft. - First Floor
1,291 Sq. Ft. - Second Floor
44,260 Cu. Ft.

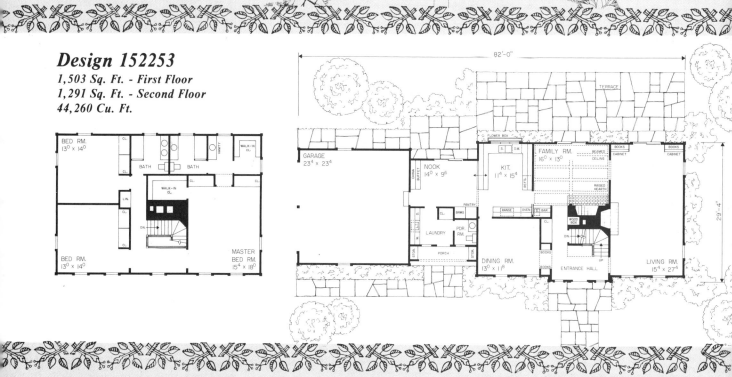

Design 152103

1,374 Sq. Ft. - First Floor
1,056 Sq. Ft. - Second Floor
36,672 Cu. Ft.

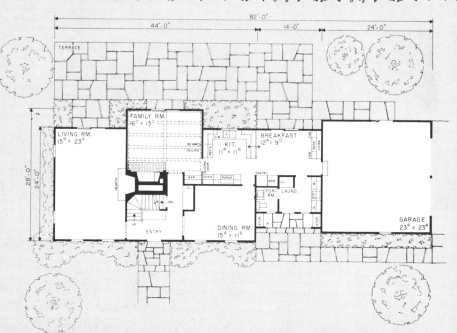

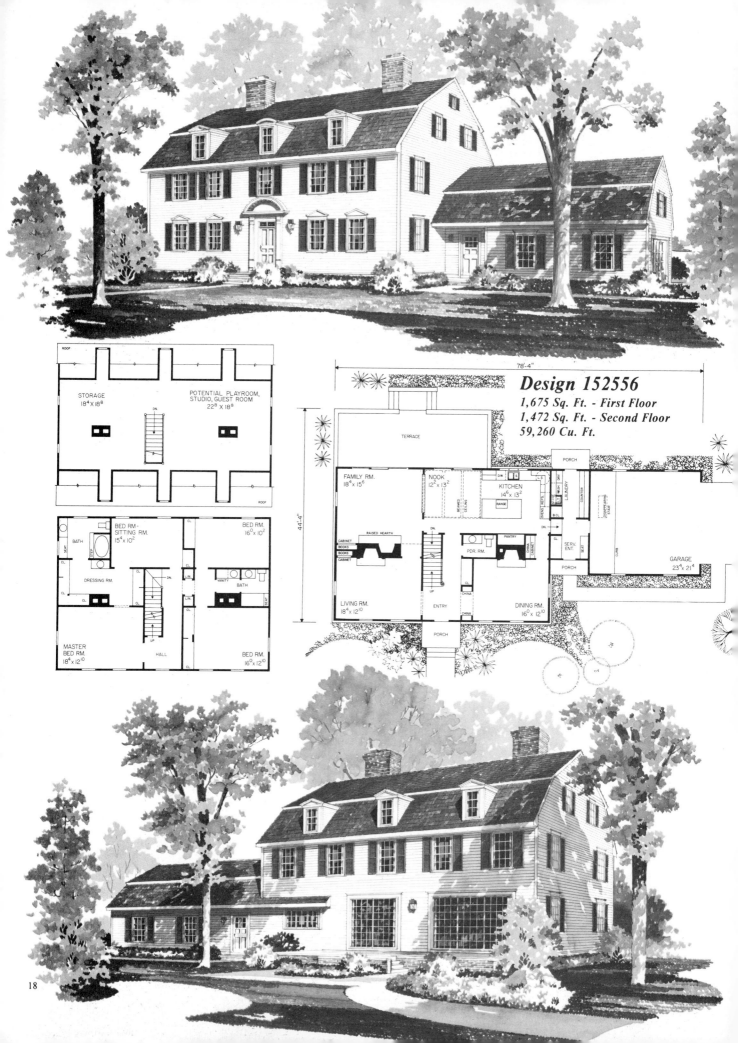

Design 152556

1,675 Sq. Ft. - First Floor
1,472 Sq. Ft. - Second Floor
59,260 Cu. Ft.

STORAGE
18⁴ X 18⁸

POTENTIAL PLAYROOM,
STUDIO, GUEST ROOM
22⁸ X 18⁸

BED RM.-
SITTING RM.
15⁴ X 10²

BED RM.
16⁰ X 10²

DRESSING RM.

BATH

VANITY

MASTER
BED RM.
18⁴ X 12¹⁰

HALL

BED RM.
16⁰ X 12¹⁰

78'-4"

44'-4"

TERRACE

PORCH

FAMILY RM.
18⁴ X 15⁶

NOOK
12⁰ X 13²

KITCHEN
14⁶ X 13²

RANGE

LAUNDRY

COUNTER

DISAPPEARING STAIR

RAISED HEARTH

CABINET
BOOKS
CABINET

PDR. RM.

PANTRY

CHINA

SERV. ENT.

GARAGE
23⁴ X 21⁴

PORCH

LIVING RM.
18⁴ X 12¹⁰

ENTRY

CHINA

DINING RM.
16⁰ X 12¹⁰

PORCH

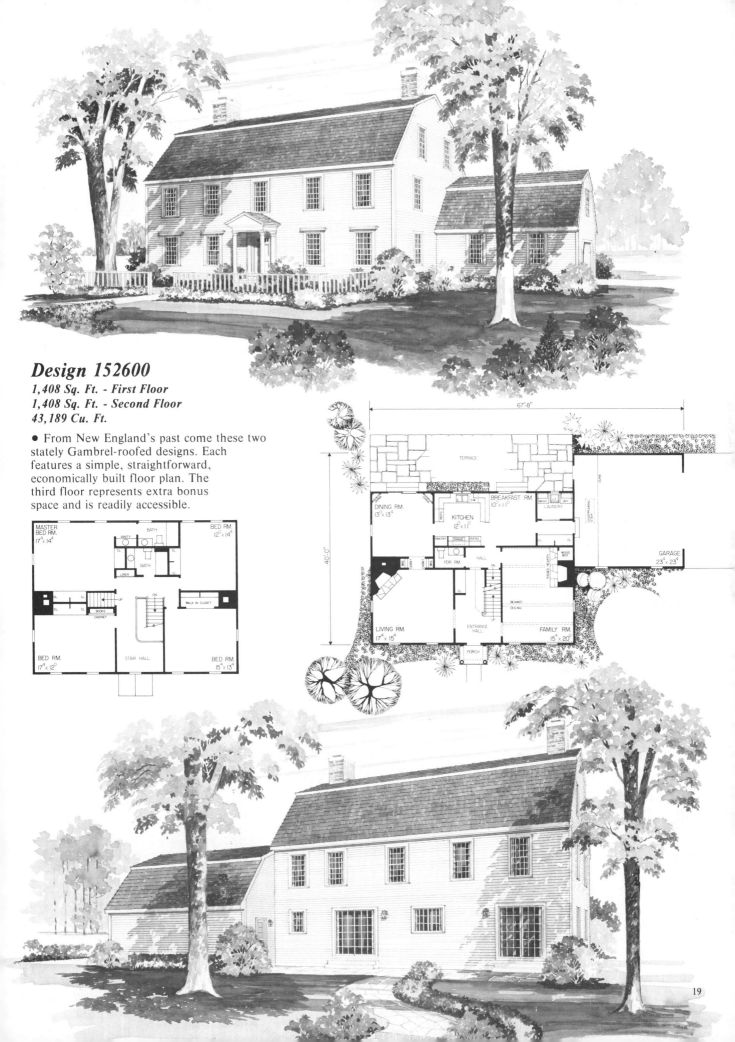

Design 152600

1,408 Sq. Ft. - First Floor
1,408 Sq. Ft. - Second Floor
43,189 Cu. Ft.

● From New England's past come these two stately Gambrel-roofed designs. Each features a simple, straightforward, economically built floor plan. The third floor represents extra bonus space and is readily accessible.

Design 152140 *1,822 Sq. Ft. - First Floor; 1,638 Sq. Ft. - Second Floor; 52,107 Cu. Ft.*

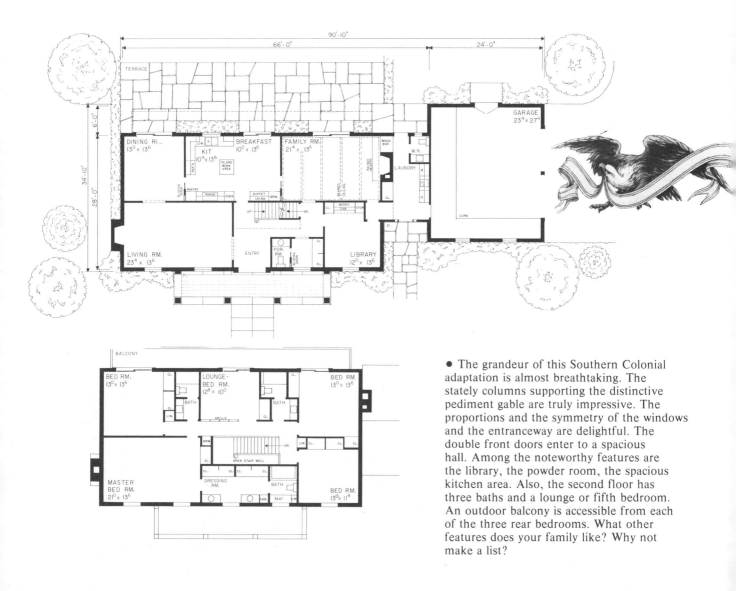

● The grandeur of this Southern Colonial adaptation is almost breathtaking. The stately columns supporting the distinctive pediment gable are truly impressive. The proportions and the symmetry of the windows and the entranceway are delightful. The double front doors enter to a spacious hall. Among the noteworthy features are the library, the powder room, the spacious kitchen area. Also, the second floor has three baths and a lounge or fifth bedroom. An outdoor balcony is accessible from each of the three rear bedrooms. What other features does your family like? Why not make a list?

Design 152700 *1,640 Sq. Ft. - First Floor; 1,129 Sq. Ft. - Second Floor; 42,000 Cu. Ft.*

● Southern Colonial grace! And much more. An elegant gathering room, more than 21' by 23' large . . . with sloped ceilings and a raised-hearth fireplace. Plus two sets of window-doors that open onto the terrace. Correctly appointed formal rooms! A living room with full length paned windows. And a formal dining room that features a large bay window. Plus a contemporary kitchen. A separate dining nook that includes another bay window. Charming and sunny! Around the corner, a first-floor laundry offers more modern convenience. Four large bedrooms! Including a master suite with two walk-in wardrobes and private bath. This home offers all the conveniences that make life easy! And it's eminently suited to a family with traditional tastes.

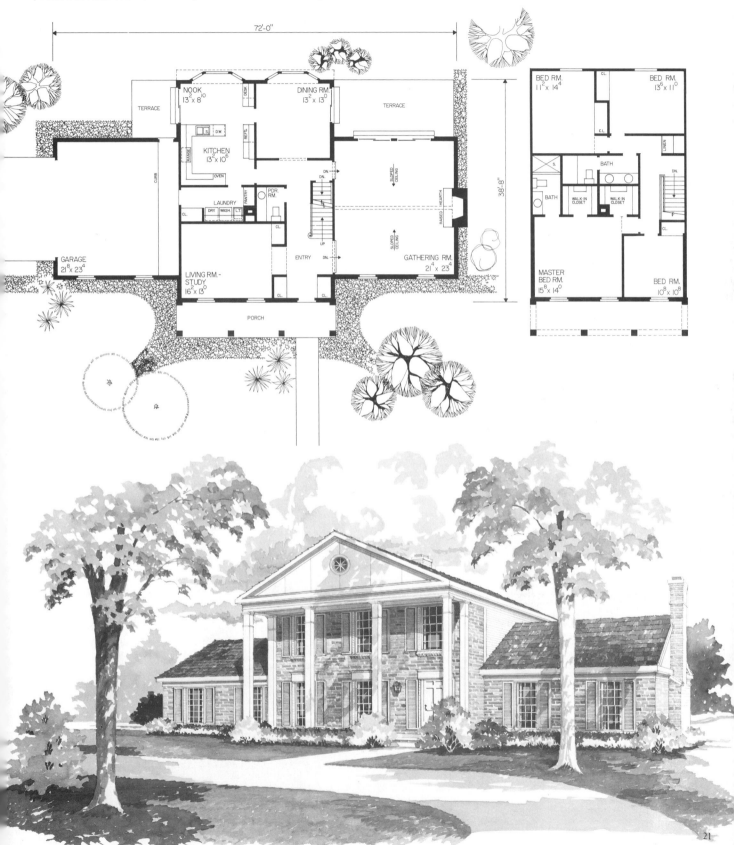

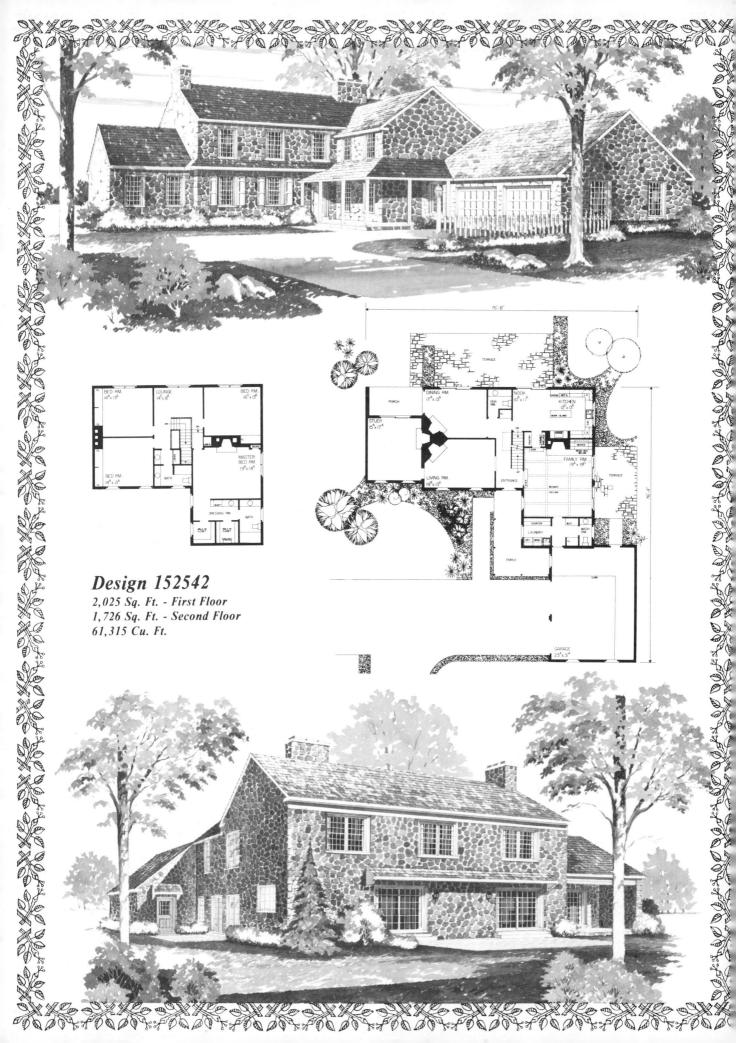

Design 152542

2,025 Sq. Ft. - First Floor
1,726 Sq. Ft. - Second Floor
61,315 Cu. Ft.

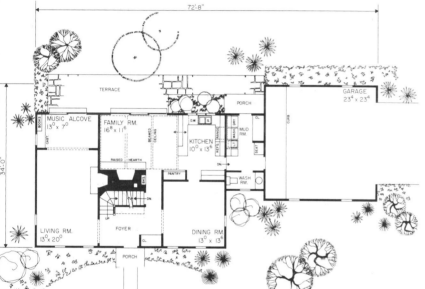

Design 152521

1,272 Sq. Ft. - First Floor
1,139 Sq. Ft. - Second Floor
37,262 Cu. Ft.

First Floor:
- MUSIC ALCOVE 13⁰ x 7⁰
- FAMILY RM. 16⁸ x 11⁶
- KITCHEN 10⁰ x 13⁶
- GARAGE 23⁴ x 23⁴
- LIVING RM. 13⁰ x 20⁰
- DINING RM. 13⁰ x 13⁶

Second Floor:
- BED RM. 13⁰ x 11⁶
- MASTER BED RM. 13⁰ x 18⁰
- BED RM. 13⁰ x 15⁶

72'-8"
34'-0"

Design 151933

1,184 Sq. Ft. - First Floor
884 Sq. Ft. - Second Floor; 27,976 Cu. Ft.

● An attractive Farmhouse adaptation
with just loads of livability. The
center entrance routes traffic
efficiently to all areas. Note
spacious end, living room and
its adjacent formal dining room.
A great family room, laundry, and
four bedroom second floor.

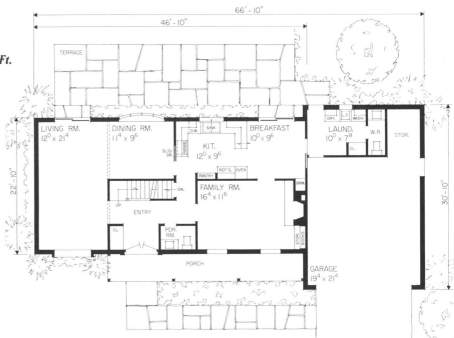

Design 152585

990 Sq. Ft. - First Floor
1,011 Sq. Ft. - Second Floor; 30,230 Cu. Ft.

● Here is an elegant version of the
front porch type house. Note the
overhanging second floor. An
efficient and economical home for
the large family.

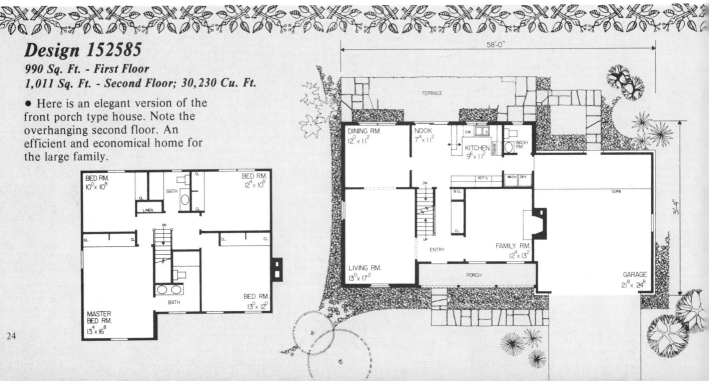

24

Design 151285

1,202 Sq. Ft. - First Floor
896 Sq. Ft. - Second Floor; 27,385 Cu. Ft.

● Designed for years of livability.
And what great livability this two-story
traditional has to offer. The spacious
center entry hall routes traffic
conveniently to all areas. The formal
living room is big and features two
windows overlooking the front yard.

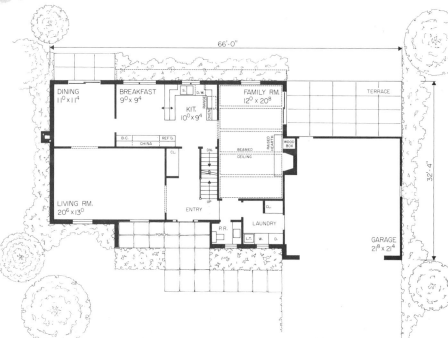

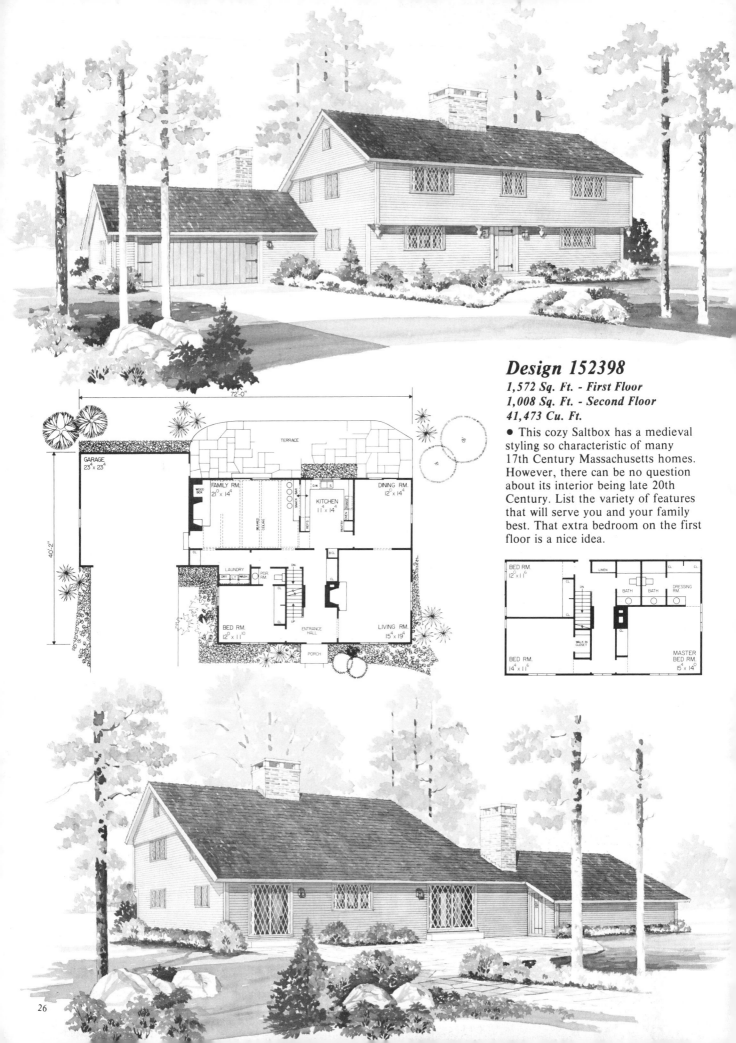

Design 152398

1,572 Sq. Ft. - First Floor
1,008 Sq. Ft. - Second Floor
41,473 Cu. Ft.

● This cozy Saltbox has a medieval styling so characteristic of many 17th Century Massachusetts homes. However, there can be no question about its interior being late 20th Century. List the variety of features that will serve you and your family best. That extra bedroom on the first floor is a nice idea.

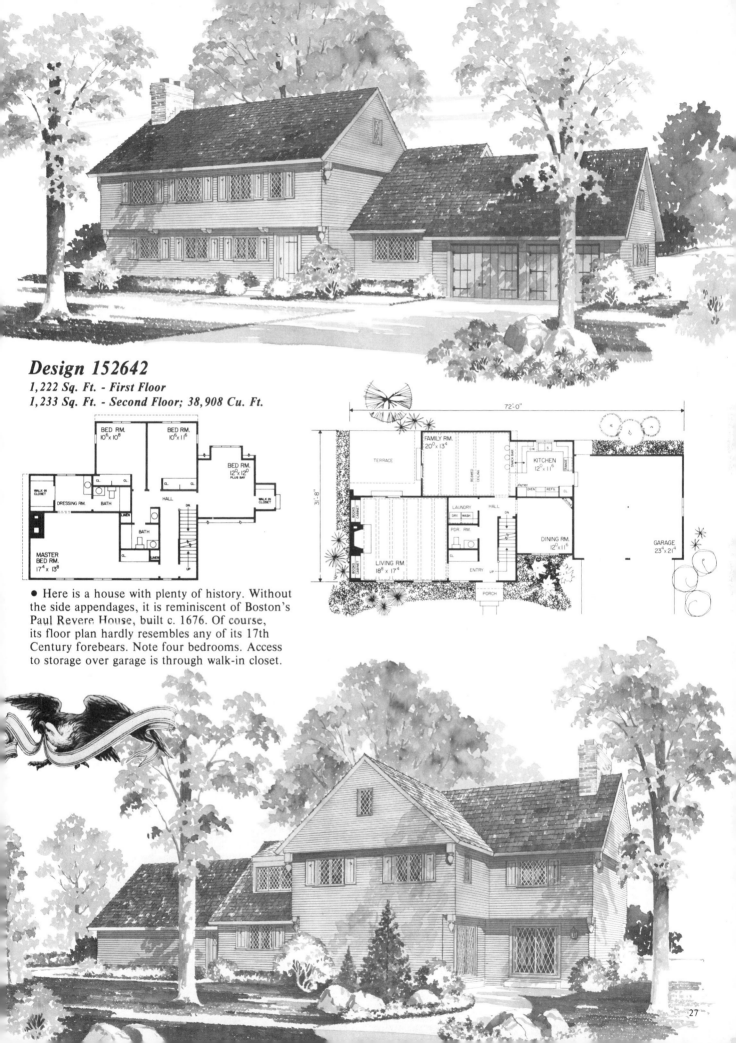

Design 152642

1,222 Sq. Ft. - First Floor
1,233 Sq. Ft. - Second Floor; 38,908 Cu. Ft.

BED RM.
10⁶ x 10⁸

BED RM.
10⁶ x 11⁶

BED RM.
12⁰ x 12⁰
PLUS BAY

WALK-IN CLOSET

WALK IN CLOSET

DRESSING RM.

BATH

HALL

CL.

LINEN

BATH

LINEN

UP

MASTER BED RM.
17⁴ x 13⁸

72'-0"

FAMILY RM.
20⁰ x 13⁴

TERRACE

KITCHEN
12⁰ x 11⁶

SNACK BAR

RANGE

PNTRY

OVEN

REF'S

CL

31'-8"

BOOKS CABINET

LIVING RM.
18⁸ x 17⁴

LAUNDRY

DRY

WASH

HALL

DN

PDR. RM.

CL

ENTRY

UP

DINING RM.
12⁰ x 11⁶

GARAGE
23⁴ x 21⁴

PORCH

● Here is a house with plenty of history. Without the side appendages, it is reminiscent of Boston's Paul Revere House, built c. 1676. Of course, its floor plan hardly resembles any of its 17th Century forebears. Note four bedrooms. Access to storage over garage is through walk-in closet.

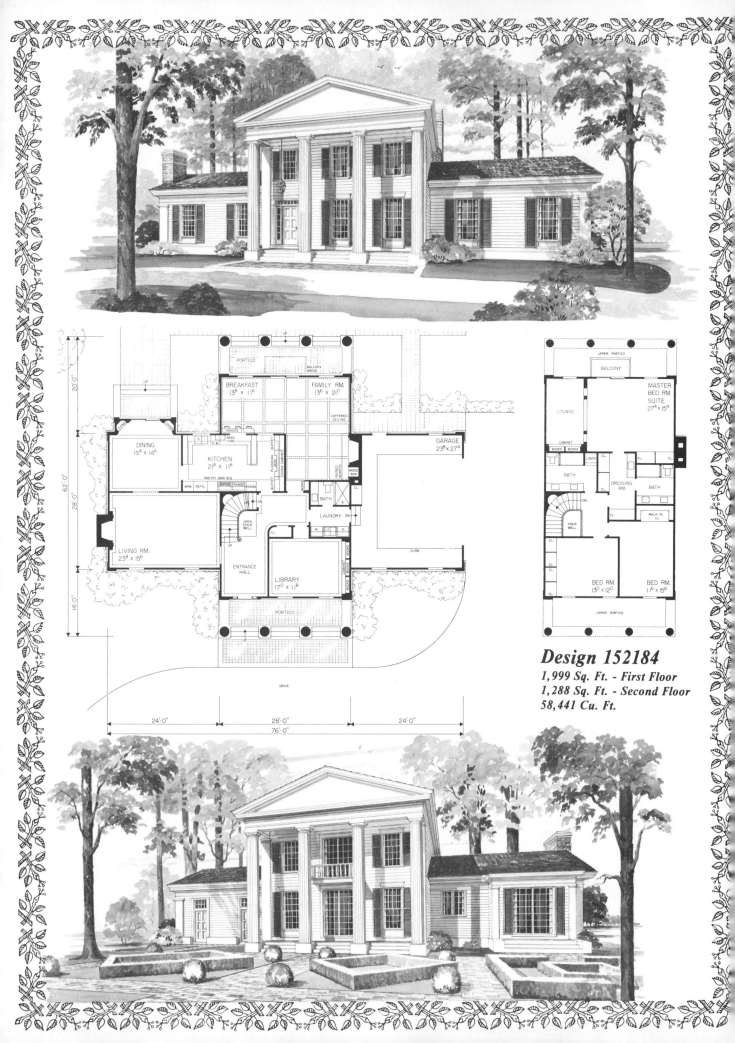

Design 152184

1,999 Sq. Ft. - First Floor
1,288 Sq. Ft. - Second Floor
58,441 Cu. Ft.

First Floor

PORTICO

BREAKFAST
13⁸ x 11⁶

FAMILY RM.
13⁶ x 21⁰

BALCONY ABOVE

COFFERED CEILING

DINING
15⁴ x 14⁶

KITCHEN
21⁸ x 11⁶

SNACKS

PASS THRU

BUFFET

PLANNING DESK

CHINA CABINET

RAISED HEARTH

GARAGE
23⁸ x 27⁴

WOOD BOX

PANTRY BAR-B-Q

BRM. REF'G. RANGE OVENS

BATH

LAUNDRY DN.

W. L.T. D.

OPEN STAIR WELL

DN.

UP

LIVING RM.
23⁸ x 15⁶

ENTRANCE HALL

LIBRARY
17⁰ x 11⁸

CABINET BOOKS

CURB

PORTICO

DRIVE

24'-0" 28'-0" 24'-0"
76'-0"

20'-0"
62'-0"
28'-0"
14'-0"

Second Floor

UPPER PORTICO

BALCONY

LOUNGE

MASTER BED RM. SUITE
27⁴ x 15⁴

CABINET BOOKS BOOKS LINEN CL.

BATH

DRESSING RM.

BATH

CL.

WALK-IN CL.

STAIR WELL

DN.

CL.
CL.
CL.

BED RM.
13⁰ x 12⁰

BED RM.
11⁶ x 15⁶

UPPER PORTICO

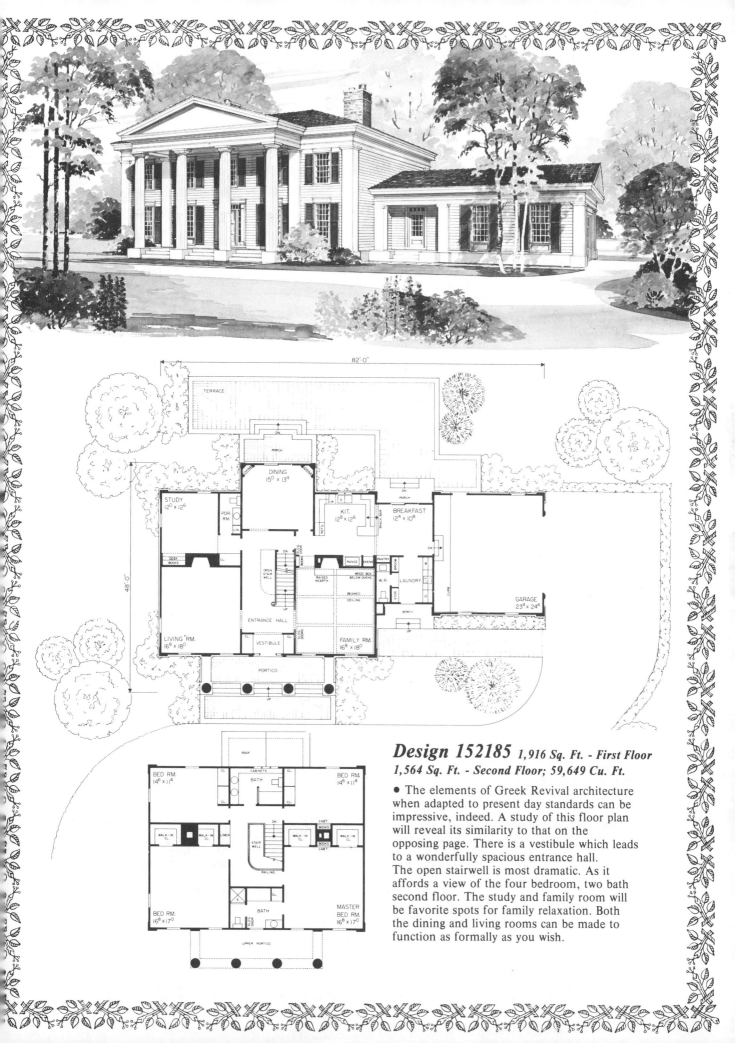

Design 152185 *1,916 Sq. Ft. - First Floor*
1,564 Sq. Ft. - Second Floor; 59,649 Cu. Ft.

● The elements of Greek Revival architecture when adapted to present day standards can be impressive, indeed. A study of this floor plan will reveal its similarity to that on the opposing page. There is a vestibule which leads to a wonderfully spacious entrance hall. The open stairwell is most dramatic. As it affords a view of the four bedroom, two bath second floor. The study and family room will be favorite spots for family relaxation. Both the dining and living rooms can be made to function as formally as you wish.

Design 151887

1,518 Sq. Ft. - First Floor
1,144 Sq. Ft. - Second Floor
40,108 Cu. Ft.

● The Gambrel roof Colonial is steeped in history. And well it should be, for its pleasing proportions are a delight to the eye. The various roof planes, the window treatment, and the rambling nature of the entire house revive a picture of rural New England. The covered porch protects the front door which opens into a spacious entrance hall. Traffic then flows in an orderly fashion to the end living room, the separate dining room, the cozy family room, and to the spacious country-kitchen. There is a first floor laundry, plenty of coat closets, and a handy powder room.

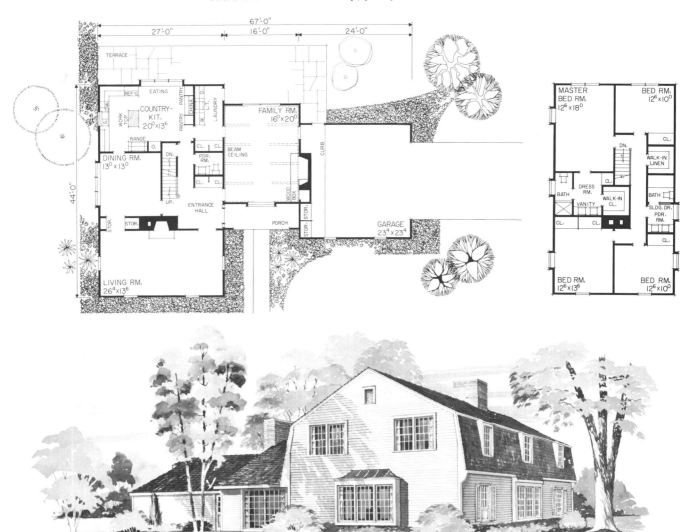

Design 152907 1,546 Sq. Ft. - First Floor; 1,144 Sq. Ft. - Second Floor; 40,750 Cu. Ft.

● This traditional L-shaped farmhouse is charming, indeed, with gambrel roof, dormer windows, and covered porch supported by slender columns and side rails. A spacious country kitchen with a bay provides a cozy gathering place for family and friends, as well as convenient place for food preparation with its central work island and size. There's a formal dining room also adjacent to the kitchen. A rear family room features its own fireplace, as does a large living room in the front. All four bedrooms are isolated upstairs, away from other household activity and noise. Included is a larger master bedroom suite with its own bath, dressing room, and abundant closet space. This is a comfortable home for the modern family who can appreciate the tradition and charm of the past.

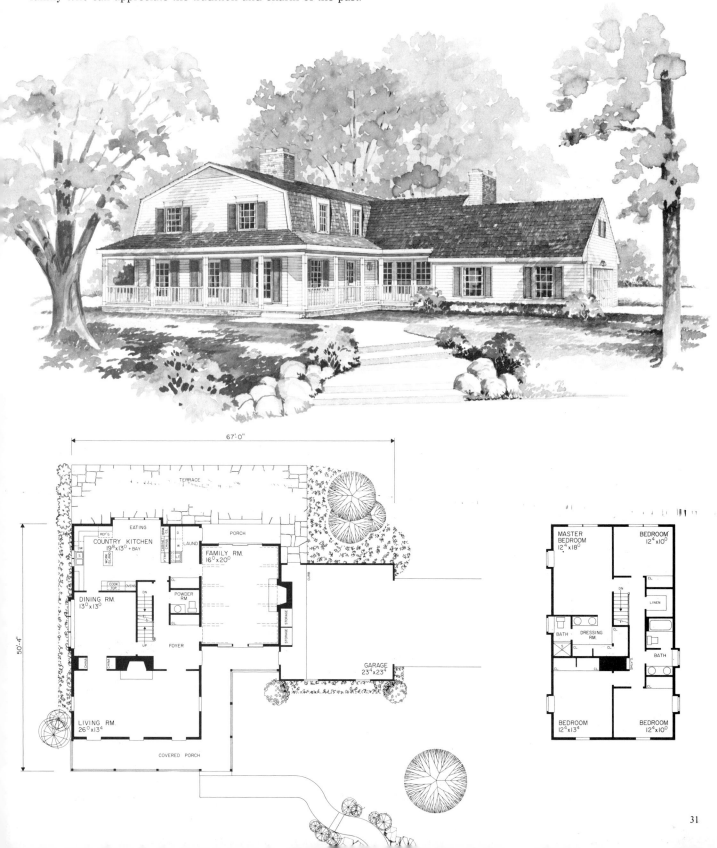

Design 152176

1,485 Sq. Ft. - First Floor
1,175 Sq. Ft. - Second Floor; 41,646 Cu. Ft.

● An appealing Georgian adaptation complete with twin chimneys, brick quoins, recessed entrance, carriage lamps, cupola and pleasing proportions. A great investment.

● You'll never regret your choice of this Georgian design. Its stately facade seems to foretell all of the exceptional features to be found inside. From the delightfully spacious front entry hall, to the studio or maid's room over the garage, this home is unique all along the way. Imagine four fireplaces, three full baths, two extra wash rooms, a family room, plus a quiet library. And there's more.

Design 151858

1,794 Sq. Ft. - First Floor
1,474 Sq. Ft. - Second Floor
424 Sq. Ft. - Studio; 54,878 Cu. Ft.

Design 152221

1,726 Sq. Ft. - First Floor
1,440 Sq. Ft. - Second Floor; 50,204 Cu. Ft.

● Another Georgian version. This time with horizontal siding. Study plan carefully. There is attic storage space over garage accessible from rear bedroom.

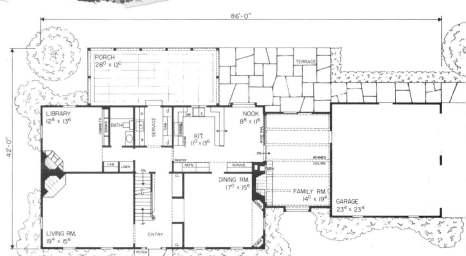

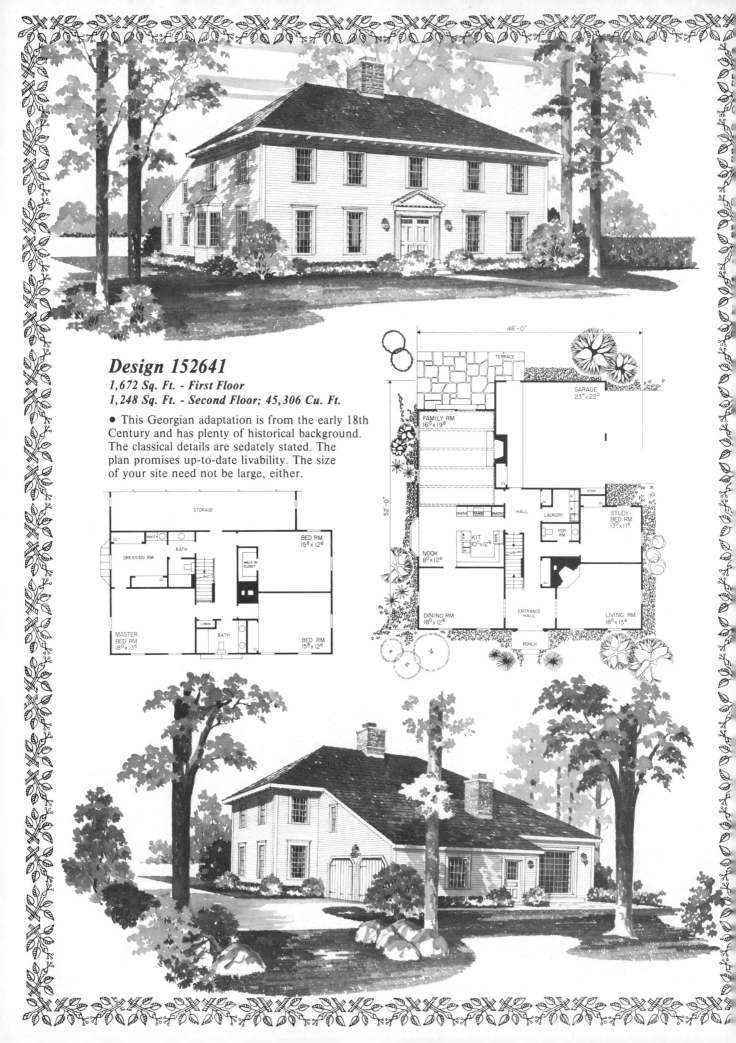

Design 152641

1,672 Sq. Ft. - First Floor
1,248 Sq. Ft. - Second Floor; 45,306 Cu. Ft.

● This Georgian adaptation is from the early 18th Century and has plenty of historical background. The classical details are sedately stated. The plan promises up-to-date livability. The size of your site need not be large, either.

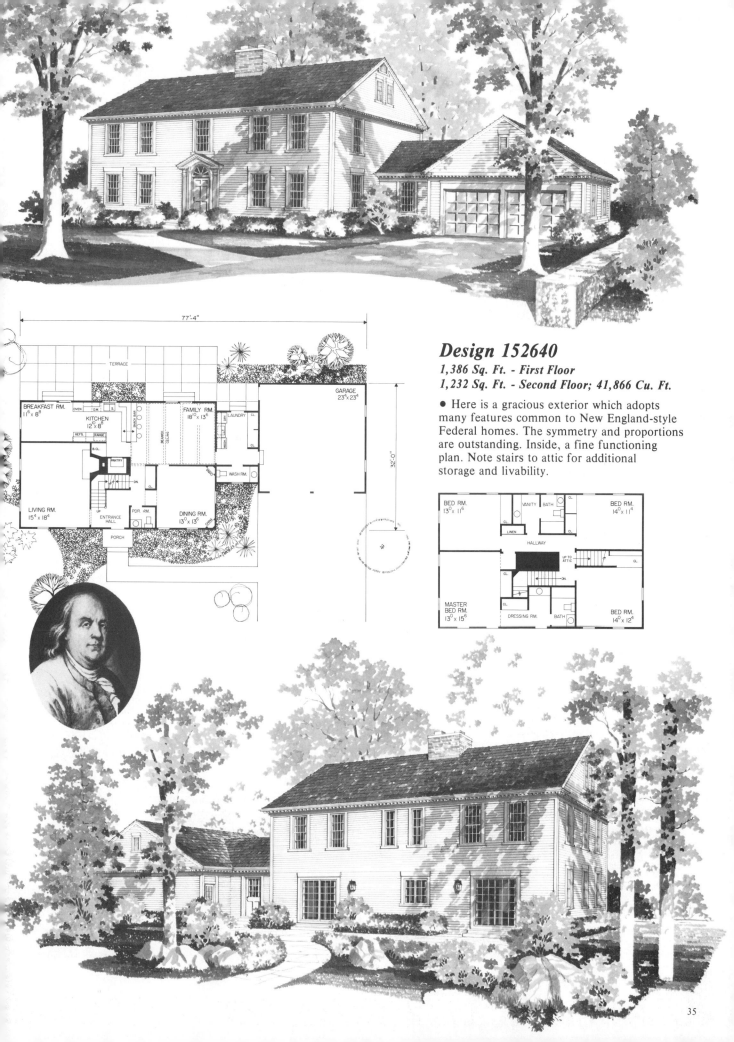

Design 152640

1,386 Sq. Ft. - First Floor
1,232 Sq. Ft. - Second Floor; 41,866 Cu. Ft.

● Here is a gracious exterior which adopts many features common to New England-style Federal homes. The symmetry and proportions are outstanding. Inside, a fine functioning plan. Note stairs to attic for additional storage and livability.

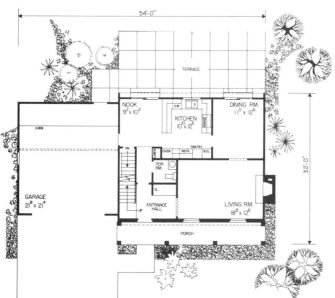

Design 152627

845 Sq. Ft. - First Floor
896 Sq. Ft. - Second Floor; 28,685 Cu. Ft.

● This charming, economically built, home with its stately porch columns is reminiscent of the South. The efficient interior features bonus space over garage and in the third-floor attic.

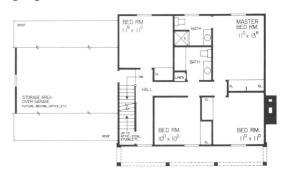

Design 152524

994 Sq. Ft. - First Floor
994 Sq. Ft. - Second Floor; 32,937 Cu. Ft.

● This small two-story with a modest investment, will result in an impressive exterior and an outstanding interior which will provide exceptional livability. Your list of features will be long.

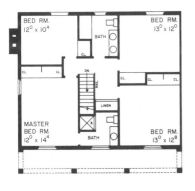

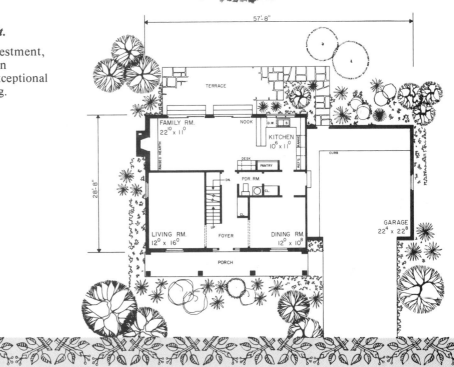

Design 152107

1,020 Sq. Ft. - First Floor
720 Sq. Ft. - Second Floor; 25,245 Cu. Ft.

● A Southern Colonial adaptation under 2,000 square feet. The two projecting wings are devoted to the living room (with covered porch) and the garage. An impressive, yet modest home.

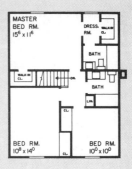

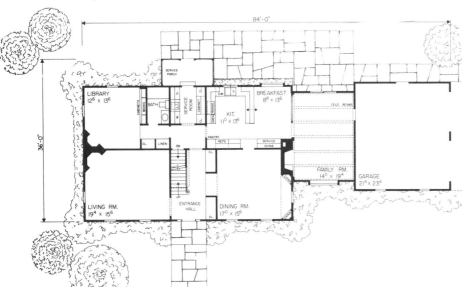

Design 152157

1,720 Sq. Ft. - First Floor
1,205 Sq. Ft. - Second Floor
40,963 Cu. Ft.

First Floor

84'-0"

36'-0"

LIBRARY
12⁶ x 13⁶

SERVICE PORCH

BATH

SERVICE ROOM

KIT.
11⁰ x 13⁶

BREAKFAST
8⁸ x 13⁶

PANTRY

CL.   LINEN

DN

UP

ENTRANCE HALL

DINING RM.
17⁰ x 15⁶

LIVING RM.
19⁴ x 15⁶

FAMILY RM.
14⁰ x 19⁴

GARAGE
21⁴ x 23⁴

Second Floor

DRESSING ROOM

VANITY

BATH   BATH

LINEN

BED RM.
14⁸ x 12⁶

MASTER BED RM.
17⁰ x 15⁶

DN

BED RM.
14⁸ x 11⁴

Design 152320 *1,856 Sq. Ft. - First Floor*
1,171 Sq. Ft. - Second Floor; 46,699 Cu. Ft.

Design 152192 *1,884 Sq. Ft. - First Floor*
1,521 Sq. Ft. - Second Floor; 58,380 Cu. Ft.

● This is surely a fine adaptation from the 18th-Century when formality and elegance were bywords. The authentic detailing of this design centers around the fine proportions, the dentils, the window symmetry, the front door and entranceway, the massive chimneys and the masonry work. The rear elevation retains all the grandeur exemplary of exquisite architecture. The appeal of this outstanding home does not end with its exterior elevations. Consider the formal living room with its corner fireplace. Also, the library with its wall of bookshelves and cabinets. Further, the dining room highlights corner china cabinets. Continue to study this elegant plan.

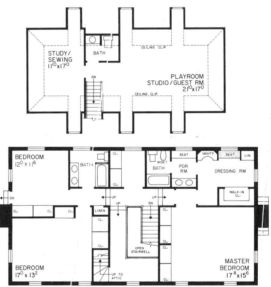

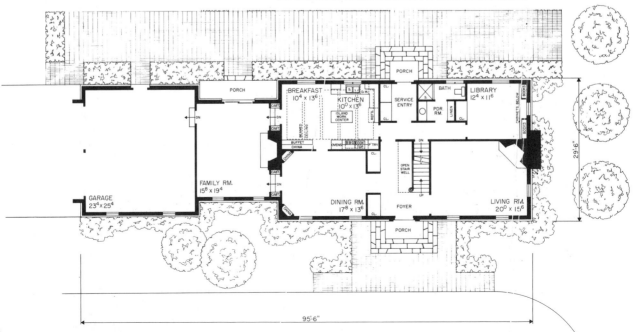

● Design 152192 - Garden View

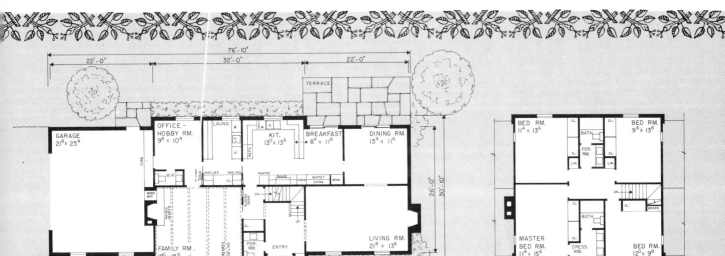

Design 152139

1,581 Sq. Ft. - First Floor
991 Sq. Ft. - Second Floor; 36,757 Cu. Ft.

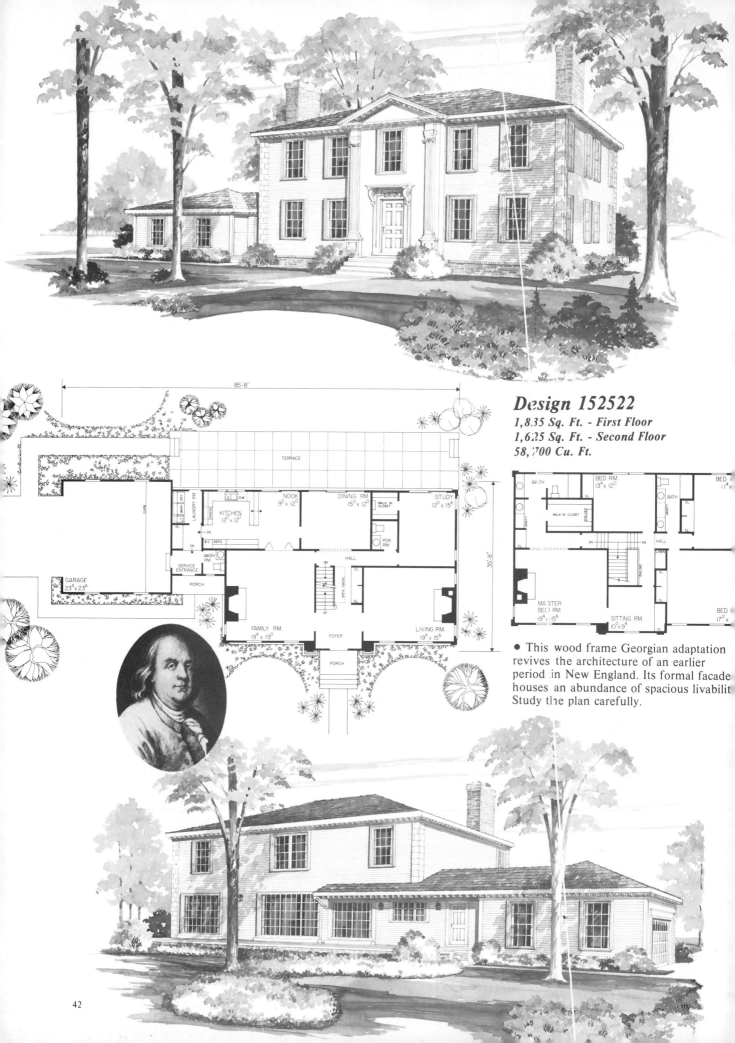

Design 152522

1,835 Sq. Ft. - First Floor
1,625 Sq. Ft. - Second Floor
58,700 Cu. Ft.

• This wood frame Georgian adaptation revives the architecture of an earlier period in New England. Its formal facade houses an abundance of spacious livabilit Study the plan carefully.

1½ StoryHomes

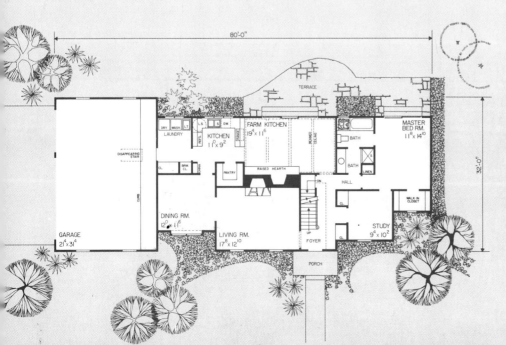

Design 152563

1,500 Sq. Ft. - First Floor
690 Sq. Ft. - Second Floor
38,243 Cu. Ft.

● This charming one-and-a-half story Cape Cod home has an interesting story to tell. It is patterned after the Historic half-houses which were originally built as a single, main structure with a door to one side of the facade. As the family grew in numbers, and the fortunes improved, various sections were successively added. The result was often a rambling house with varying roof planes and interesting appendages. The interior of this delightful design will surely cater ideally to the needs of the active, modern family. Don't miss the cozy farm kitchen area with its raised hearth fireplace and beamed ceiling. Note the study and the upstairs sitting room, Also, the laundry, walk-in pantry and all that attic storage. This design has a basement, too.

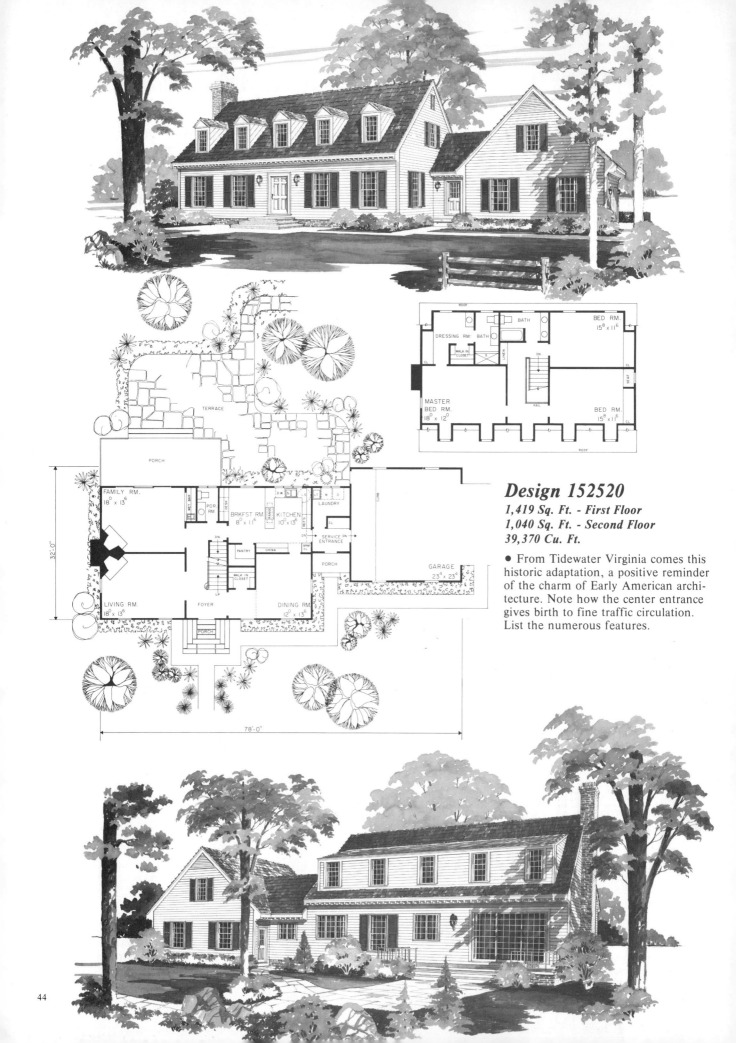

Design 152520

1,419 Sq. Ft. - First Floor
1,040 Sq. Ft. - Second Floor
39,370 Cu. Ft.

● From Tidewater Virginia comes this historic adaptation, a positive reminder of the charm of Early American architecture. Note how the center entrance gives birth to fine traffic circulation. List the numerous features.

Design 151970

1,664 Sq. Ft. - First Floor
1,116 Sq. Ft. - Second Floor
41,912 Cu. Ft.

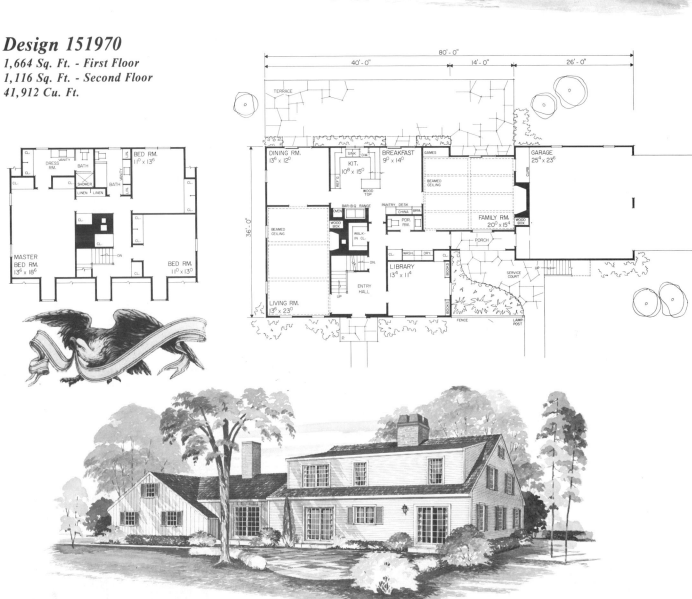

• The prototype of this Colonial house was an integral part of the 18th-Century New England landscape; the updated version is a welcome addition to any suburban scene. Main entry wing, patterned after classic Cape Cod cottage design, is two stories high but has a pleasing groundhugging look. Steeply pitched roof, triple dormers, massive central chimney anchor the house firmly to its site. Front elevation is symmetrically balanced; doorway, middle dormer, and chimney are in perfect alignment. One-story wide, the windowed wing leading to the garage is a spacious beam-ceilinged family room with splay-walled entry porch on front, sliding glass window at rear.

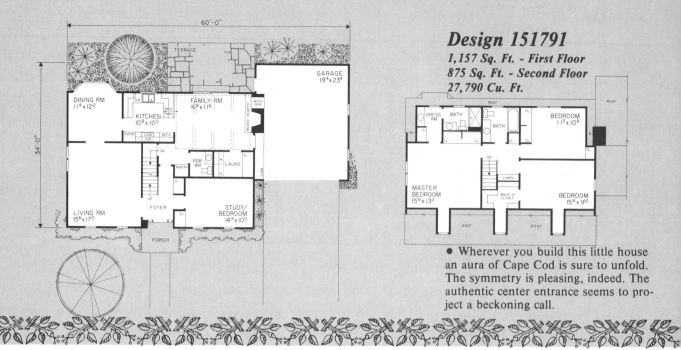

Design 151791
1,157 Sq. Ft. - First Floor
875 Sq. Ft. - Second Floor
27,790 Cu. Ft.

● Wherever you build this little house an aura of Cape Cod is sure to unfold. The symmetry is pleasing, indeed. The authentic center entrance seems to project a beckoning call.

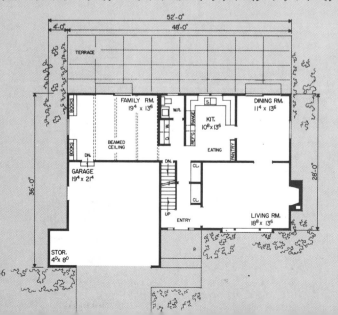

● You don't need a mansion to live graciously. What you do need is a practical floor plan which takes into consideration the varied activities of the busy family. This story-and-a-half design will not require a large piece of property; for all its tremendous living potential it will return the maximum per construction dollar.

Design 151241
1,064 Sq. Ft. - First Floor
898 Sq. Ft. - Second Floor; 24,723 Cu. Ft.

46

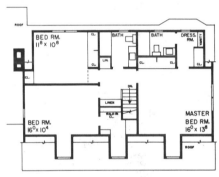

Design 152124

1,176 Sq. Ft. - First Floor
922 Sq. Ft. - Second Floor; 29,854 Cu. Ft.

● Traditional charm on a modest budget.
Here is a delightfully proportioned
1½-story house, loaded with livability,
that will build most economically.
Consider all the features carefully.

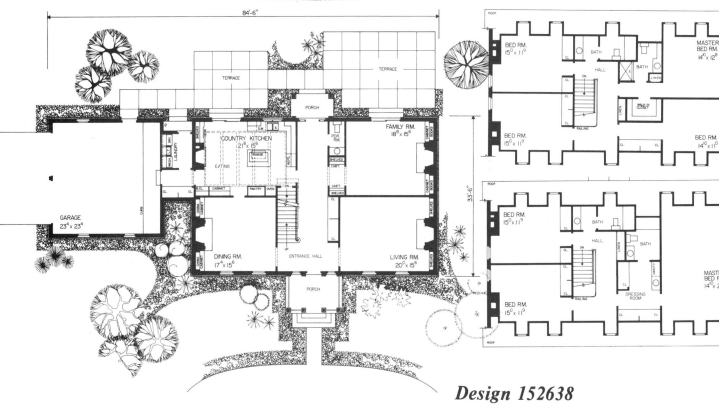

84'-6"

33'-6"

TERRACE

TERRACE

PORCH

COUNTRY KITCHEN
21'8 x 15'6

EATING

RANGE

FAMILY RM.
18'8 x 15'6

PDR.
RM.

CABINET
BOOKS

LAUNDRY

GARAGE
23'4 x 23'4

CABINET

PANTRY OVEN

CABINET
BOOKS

SHELVES

DINING RM.
17'4 x 15'6

ENTRANCE HALL

LIVING RM.
20'0 x 15'6

UP

PORCH

ROOF

BED RM.
15'0 x 11'9

BATH

MASTER
BED RM.
14'0 x 12'8

HALL

BATH

LINEN

BED RM.
15'0 x 11'9

RAILING

WALK IN
CLOSET

BED RM.
14'10 x 11'9

ROOF

BED RM.
15'0 x 11'9

BATH

HALL

BATH

LINEN

BED RM.
15'0 x 11'9

RAILING

DRESSING
ROOM

VANITY

MASTER
BED RM.
14'10 x 24

ROOF

Design 152638
1,836 Sq. Ft. - First Floor
1,323 Sq. Ft. - Second Floor; 57,923 Cu. Ft.

Design 152132

1,958 Sq. Ft. - First Floor
1,305 Sq. Ft. - Second Floor
51,428 Cu. Ft.

● Another Georgian adaptation with a great heritage dating back to 18th Century America. Exquisite and symmetrical detailing set the character of this impressive home. Don't overlook such features as the two fireplaces, the laundry, the beamed ceiling, the built-in china cabinets, and the oversized garage.

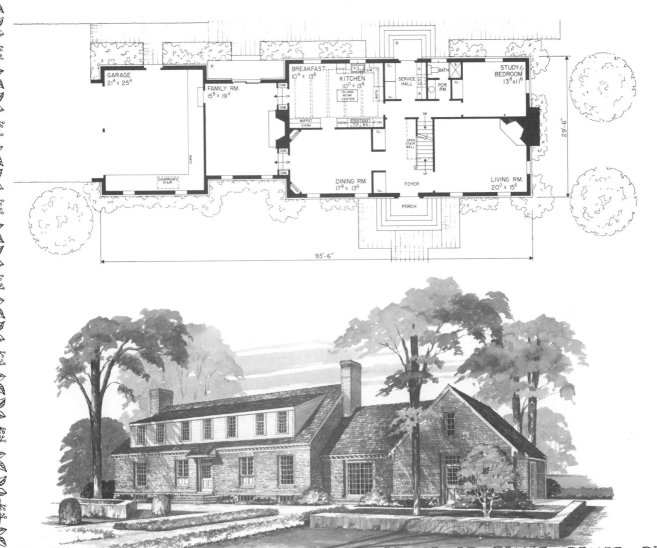

Design 152513

1,799 Sq. Ft. - First Floor
1,160 Sq. Ft. - Second Floor; 47,461 Cu. Ft.

● What an appealing story-and-a-half design - both indoors and out. The Colonial detailing of the garage is delightful, indeed. It's practical, too. There is plenty of storage space overhead. The entry hall with its open curving staircase is dramatic. Note two studies.

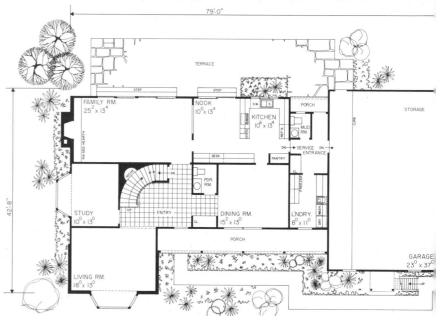

Design 152722 2,330 Sq. Ft. - First Floor

921 Sq. Ft. - Second Floor; 60,075 Cu. Ft.

● Here is a charming adaptation with extremely interesting roof lines and appendages. Imagine, an upstairs lounge overlooking both entry and gathering room. Livability, galore!

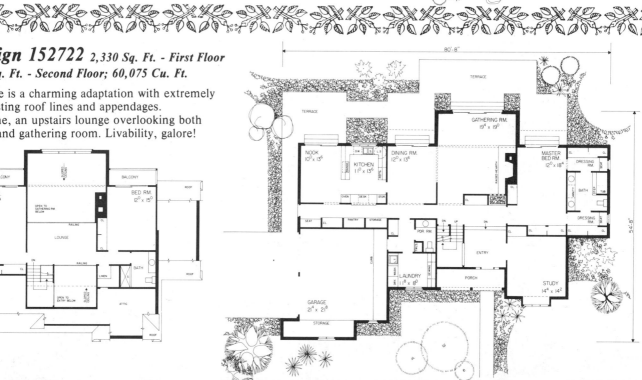

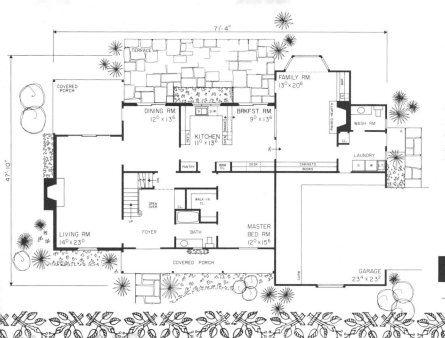

Design 152500

1,851 Sq. Ft. - First Floor
762 Sq. Ft. - Second Floor; 43,052 Cu. Ft.

● What an eye-catcher this home is! Its exterior proportions and architectural detailing are captivating, indeed. Imagine, two covered porches. Inside, the features are almost endless. The master bedroom is on the first floor with three more upstairs.

Design 152395

1,481 Sq. Ft. - First Floor
861 Sq. Ft. - Second Floor; 34,487 Cu. Ft.

● New England revisited. The appeal of this type of home is ageless. As for its livability, it will serve its occupants admirably for generations to come. With two bedrooms downstairs, you may want to finish off the second floor at a later date.

MASTER BED RM. 15⁶ x 12⁶

BED RM. 12⁴ x 14⁶

ALCOVE
BATH
BATH
ALCOVE
STAIR HALL
LINEN
DN
RAILING
CL
CL
OPEN
WALK IN CLOSET
ROOF

88'-0"

GARAGE 23⁴ x 29⁴

TERRACE

BED RM. 11⁰ x 11²

FAMILY RM. 20⁰ x 13⁰

KITCHEN 11⁴ x 17⁶

WASH RM.

LAUNDRY RM.

BATH

RAISED HEARTH

NOOK

PORCH

STORAGE

39'-0"

BED RM. 15⁶ x 11⁶

ENTRANCE HALL

LIVING RM. 21⁰ x 11⁶

PORCH

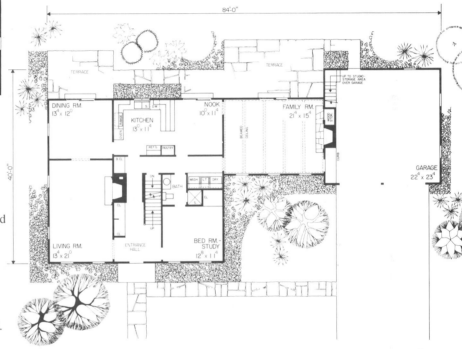

Design 152396

1,616 Sq. Ft. - First Floor; 993 Sq. Ft. - Second Floor; 30,583 Cu. Ft.

• Another picturesque facade right from the pages of our Colonial heritage. The authentic features are many. Note the centered front door with its flanking shutters, the evenly spaced dormers, and the centered chimney. The window detailing, the horizontal siding and the carriage lamps are pleasing highlights. Inside, there is exceptional livability. Observe the spacious living areas, the flexible dining facilities, the fine bedroom and bath potential. Don't miss the stairs to area over garage.

Design 152174

1,506 Sq. Ft. - First Floor
1,156 Sq. Ft. - Second Floor; 37,360 Cu. Ft.

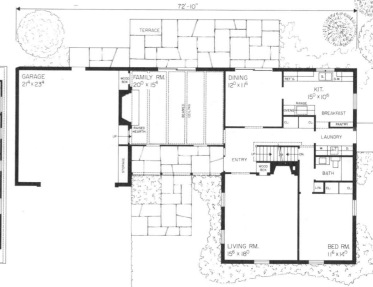

• Your building budget could hardly buy more charm, or greater livability. The appeal of the exterior is wrapped up in a myriad of design features. List them.

Design 152757

2,052 Sq. Ft. - First Floor
1,425 Sq. Ft. - Second Floor; 56,775 Cu. Ft.

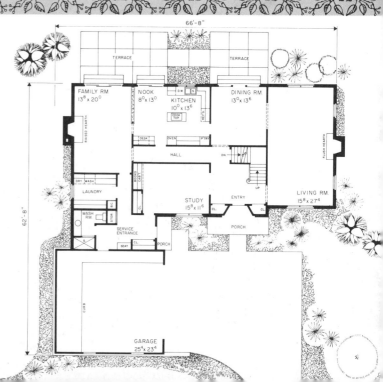

• An L-shaped story-and-a-half with a traditional facade is hard to beat for pure charm. Imagine how the living patterns will cater to the needs of your family.

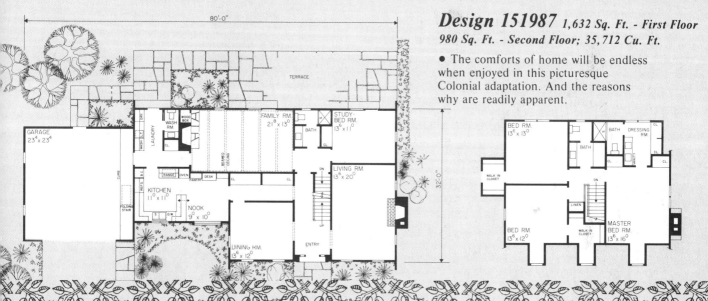

Design 151987 *1,632 Sq. Ft. - First Floor*
980 Sq. Ft. - Second Floor; 35,712 Cu. Ft.

● The comforts of home will be endless
when enjoyed in this picturesque
Colonial adaptation. And the reasons
why are readily apparent.

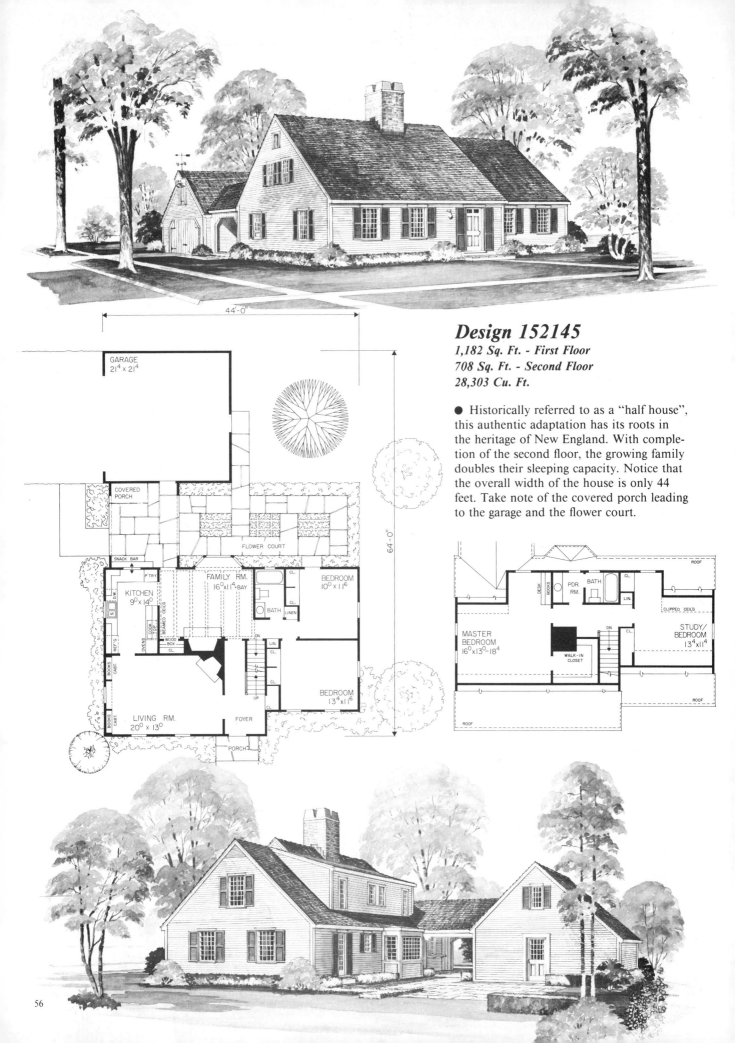

Design 152145

1,182 Sq. Ft. - First Floor
708 Sq. Ft. - Second Floor
28,303 Cu. Ft.

● Historically referred to as a "half house", this authentic adaptation has its roots in the heritage of New England. With completion of the second floor, the growing family doubles their sleeping capacity. Notice that the overall width of the house is only 44 feet. Take note of the covered porch leading to the garage and the flower court.

First Floor Plan labels:
GARAGE 21⁴ x 21⁴
COVERED PORCH
FLOWER COURT
SNACK BAR
KITCHEN 9⁰ x 14⁰
P'TRY
FAMILY RM. 16⁰ x 11⁴·BAY
BEAMED CEIL'G
COOK TOP
OVENS
WOOD BOX
REF'G.
CABT.
BOOKS
BEDROOM 10⁰ x 11⁶
BATH
LINEN
CL.
LIN.
UP
BEDROOM 13⁴ x 11⁶
LIVING RM. 20⁰ x 13⁰
FOYER
PORCH
44'-0"
64'-0"

Second Floor Plan labels:
MASTER BEDROOM 16⁰ x 13⁰-18⁴
WALK-IN CLOSET
DESK
BOOKS
PDR. RM.
BATH
CL.
LIN.
DN
STUDY/ BEDROOM 13⁴ x 11⁴
CLIPPED CEIL'G
ROOF

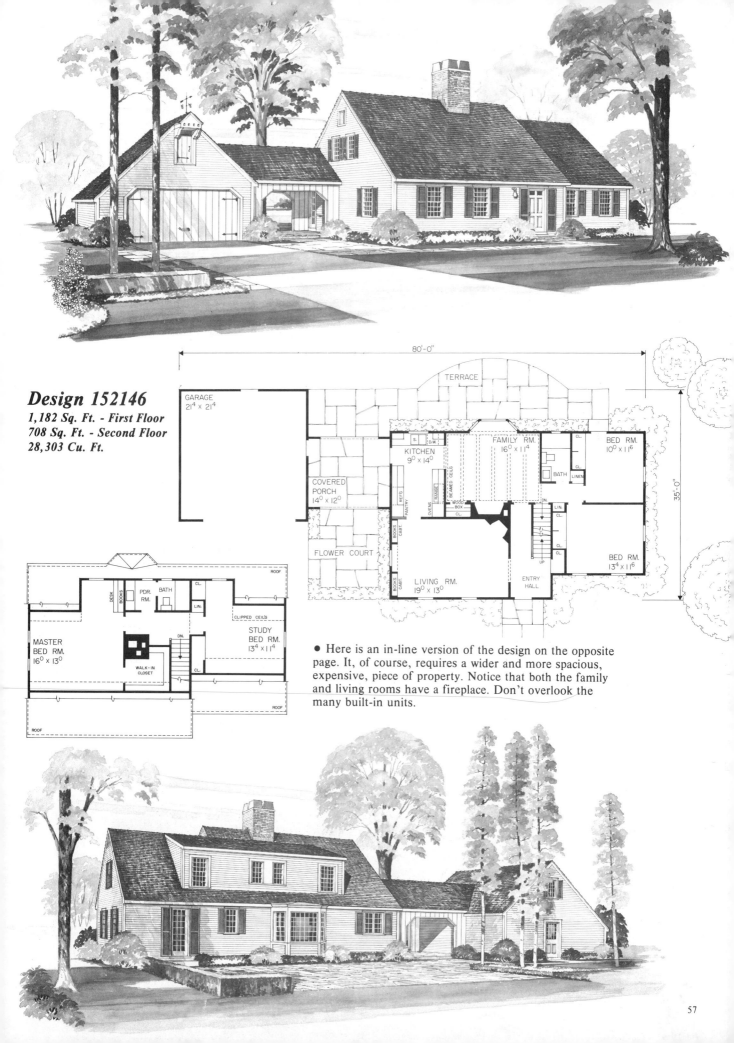

Design 152146

1,182 Sq. Ft. - First Floor
708 Sq. Ft. - Second Floor
28,303 Cu. Ft.

GARAGE
21⁴ x 21⁴

COVERED PORCH
14⁰ x 12⁰

FLOWER COURT

TERRACE

KITCHEN
9⁰ x 14⁰

FAMILY RM.
16⁰ x 11⁴

BED RM.
10⁰ x 11⁶

BATH
LINEN

BEAMED CEIL'G

WOOD BOX

OVENS
RANGE
REF'G.
PANTRY
CABT.
BOOKS

UP
DN.

LIVING RM.
19⁰ x 13⁰

ENTRY HALL

BED RM.
13⁴ x 11⁶

80'-0"

35'-0"

MASTER BED RM.
16⁰ x 13⁰

WALK-IN CLOSET

DESK
BOOKS
PDR. RM.
BATH
CL.
LIN.

CLIPPED CEIL'G

STUDY BED RM.
13⁴ x 11⁴

ROOF
DN.

● Here is an in-line version of the design on the opposite page. It, of course, requires a wider and more spacious, expensive, piece of property. Notice that both the family and living rooms have a fireplace. Don't overlook the many built-in units.

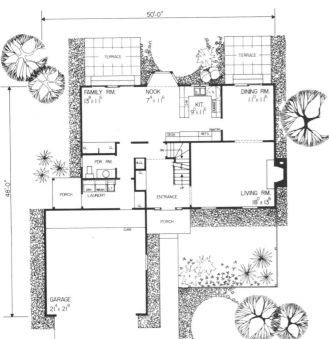

Design 152569

1,102 Sq. Ft. - First Floor
764 Sq. Ft. - Second Floor; 29,600 Cu. Ft.

● What an enchanting updated version of the popular Cape Cod cottage. There are facilities for both formal and informal living pursuits. Note the spacious family/nook area, the fine, formal dining room/living room relationship, the sliding doors to terraces, the first floor laundry, and the efficient kitchen.

Design 152162

741 Sq. Ft. - First Floor
504 Sq. Ft. - Second Floor; 17,895 Cu. Ft.

● This economical design delivers great exterior appeal and fine livability. In addition to kitchen eating space there is a separate dining room.

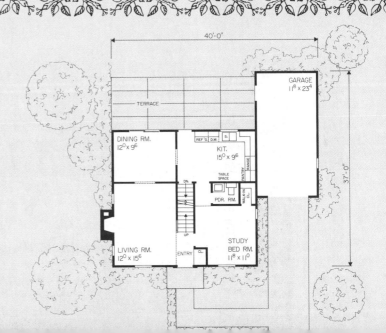

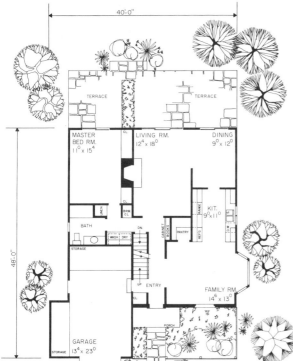

40'-0"

48'-0"

TERRACE

TERRACE

MASTER BED RM. 11⁰ x 15⁴

LIVING RM. 12⁴ x 18⁰

DINING 9⁰ x 12⁰

BATH

KIT. 9⁰ x 11⁰

STORAGE

WASH DRY

PANTRY

ENTRY

FAMILY RM. 14⁶ x 13⁰

PORCH

GARAGE 13⁴ x 23⁰

STORAGE

Design 152510 *1,191 Sq. Ft. - First Floor*
533 Sq. Ft. - Second Floor; 27,500 Cu. Ft.

● The pleasant in-line kitchen is flanked by a separate dining room and a family room. The master bedroom is on the first floor with two more bedrooms upstairs. Sliding glass doors across the rear allow for the greatest possible enjoyment of the terrace areas. Note laundry area.

ATTIC

CL

BATH

LINEN

WALK IN CL

BED RM. 13⁴ x 13⁸

DN. RAILING

BED RM. 14⁶ x 13⁸

UPPER ENTRY

ATTIC

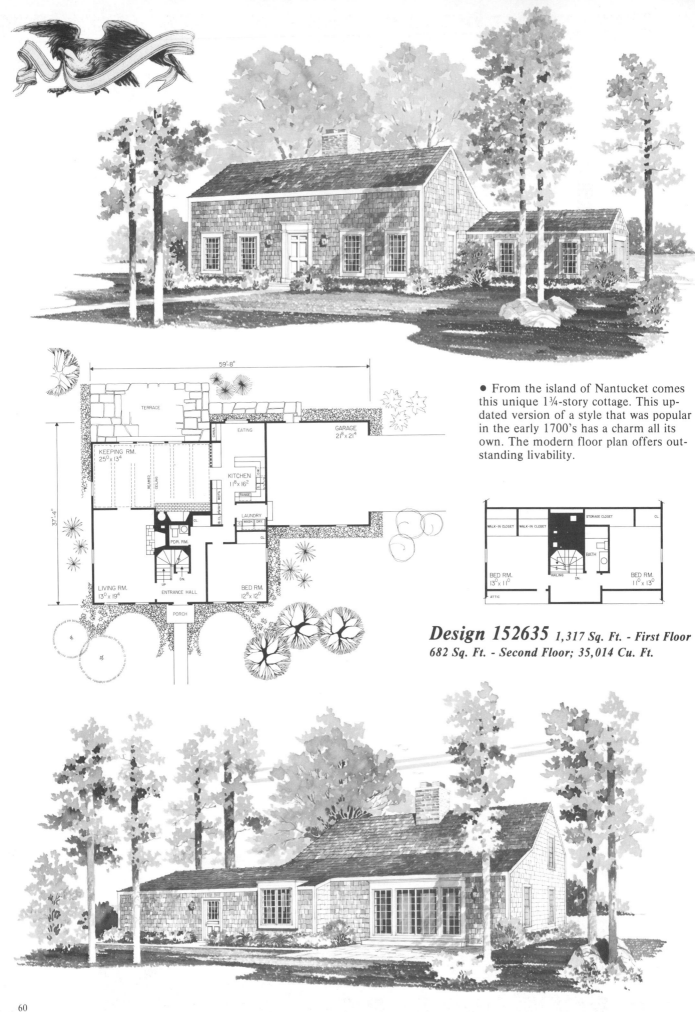

• From the island of Nantucket comes this unique 1¾-story cottage. This updated version of a style that was popular in the early 1700's has a charm all its own. The modern floor plan offers outstanding livability.

Design 152635 *1,317 Sq. Ft. - First Floor*
682 Sq. Ft. - Second Floor; 35,014 Cu. Ft.

TERRACE

KEEPING RM.
25⁰ x 13⁴

GARAGE
21⁸ x 21⁴

EATING

KITCHEN
11⁸ x 16²

RANGE

LAUNDRY
WASH DRY

PDR. RM.

UP   DN.

LIVING RM.
13⁰ x 19⁴

ENTRANCE HALL

BED RM.
12⁸ x 12⁰

PORCH

59'-8"

37'-4"

WALK-IN CLOSET   WALK-IN CLOSET

STORAGE CLOSET   CL.

BED RM.
13⁰ x 11⁰

BATH

RAILING   DN.

BED RM.
11⁰ x 13⁰

ATTIC

● Another 1¾-story home - a type of house favored by many of Cape Cod's early whalers. The compact floor plan will be economical to build and surely an energy saver. An excellent house to finish-off in stages.

STORAGE

MASTER BED RM.
16⁴ x 14⁸

BATH

LINEN

BED RM.
12⁸ x 13⁴

HALL

DN.

WALK IN CLOSET

CL

STORAGE

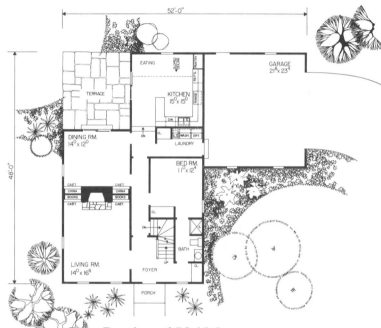

52'-0"

48'-0"

TERRACE

EATING

KITCHEN
15⁰ x 15⁰

PANTRY

REF.

RANGE

GARAGE
21⁸ x 23⁴

DINING RM.
14⁰ x 12⁰

LAUNDRY

WASH. DRY.

ON

D.W.

BED RM.
11⁰ x 12⁴

CAB'T

CHINA

BOOKS

CAB'T

CAB'T

CHINA

BOOKS

CAB'T

CL

DN.

UP

BATH

LIVING RM.
14⁰ x 16⁶

FOYER

CL

PORCH

Design 152636 *1,211 Sq. Ft. - First Floor*
747 Sq. Ft. - Second Floor; 28,681 Cu. Ft.

Design 152559

1,388 Sq. Ft. - First Floor
809 Sq. Ft. - Second Floor
36,400 Cu. Ft.

● Imagine, a 26 foot living room with fireplace, a quiet study with built-in bookshelves, and excellent dining facilities. Within such an appealing exterior, too.

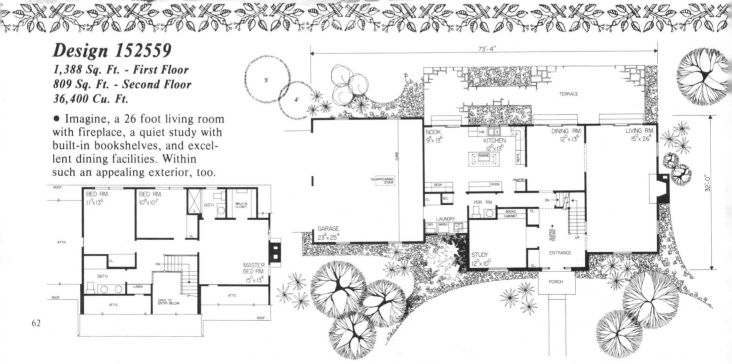

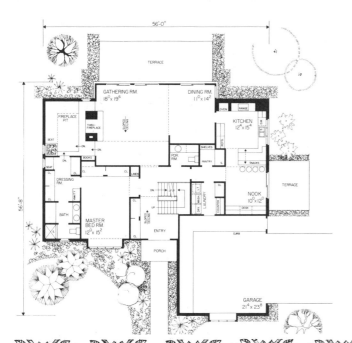

Design 152718

1,941 Sq. Ft. - First Floor
791 Sq. Ft. - Second Floor; 49,895 Cu. Ft.

● You and your family will just love the new living patterns you'll experience in this story-and-a-half home. Notice the sunken fireplace conversational pit. Don't miss the lounge which looks down on the gathering room. Then, there's the pleasant nook, efficient kitchen and master bedroom suite.

Design 152724

2,543 Sq. Ft. - First Floor
884 Sq. Ft. - Second Floor; 53,640 Cu. Ft.

● An impressive one-story front exterior with a rear dormer projecting from the second floor to provide that extra space of two, big bedrooms plus baths. Note study and lounge area.

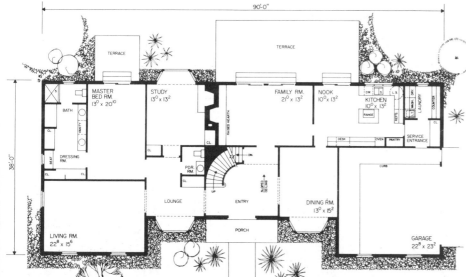

63

● Cost efficient space! That's the bonus with this attractive Cape Cod. Start in the living room . . . spacious and inviting with full-length paned windows. In the formal dining room, a bay window adds the appropriate touch. For more living space, a delightfully appointed family room . . . full-length paned windows and a traditional fireplace, plus a snack bar for casual meals! An efficient kitchen! With a pass-through to the family room and a large storage pantry. Three bedrooms.

Design 152571
1,137 Sq. Ft. - First Floor
795 Sq. Ft. - Second Floor; 28,097 Cu. Ft.

● Captivating as a New England village! From the weathervane atop the garage to the roofed side entry and paned windows, this home is perfectly detailed. With lots of living space inside! An exceptionally large family room . . . more than 29' by 13' including a dining area. A raised-hearth fireplace, too, and double doors onto the terrace. The adjoining kitchen features an island range plus cabinets, a built-in oven and lots of counter space. Attractive and efficient! Steps away, a first-floor laundry. Formal rooms, too!

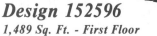

Design 152596
1,489 Sq. Ft. - First Floor
982 Sq. Ft. - Second Floor; 38,800 Cu. Ft.

One Story Homes

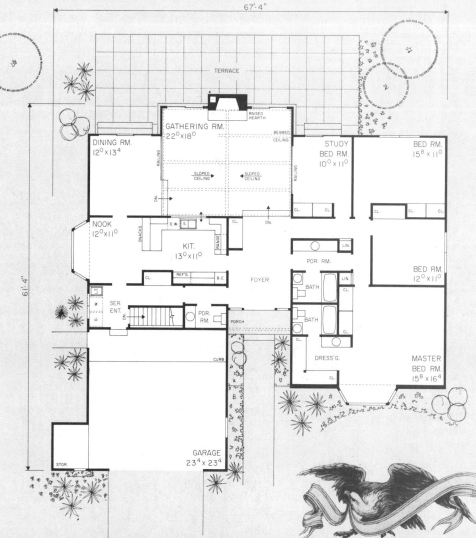

TERRACE

GATHERING RM.
22⁰x18⁰

RAISED HEARTH

BEAMED CEILING

DINING RM.
12⁰x13⁴

SLOPED CEILING SLOPED CEILING

STUDY
BED RM.
10⁰x11⁰

BED RM.
15⁸x11⁰

NOOK
12⁰x11⁰

KIT.
13⁰x11⁰

PDR. RM.

BED RM.
12⁰x11⁰

REF'G.

FOYER

BATH

BATH

SER. ENT.

PDR. RM.

PORCH

DRESS'G.

MASTER
BED RM.
15⁸x16⁴

CURB

GARAGE
23⁴x23⁴

STOR.

67'-4"

61'-4"

Design 152527

2,392 Sq. Ft.; 42,579 Cu. Ft.

● This U-shaped charmer is a good example of a maximum utilization of space to produce an abundance of livability for orientation on a relatively narrow site. Projecting the two-car garage to the front not only adds to the interest and appeal of this design, but it also reduces the size of the lot required. The zoning in this home is indeed, excellent. The spacious central foyer is but a step from the main areas. The sunken gathering room, with its sloping beamed ceiling, raised hearth fireplace, and openings to the dining room, study and kitchen, represents a true family living room. The inside kitchen is handy to all areas. Study the excellent sleeping zone. Note two full baths.

Design 152505

1,366 Sq. Ft.; 29,329 Cu. Ft.

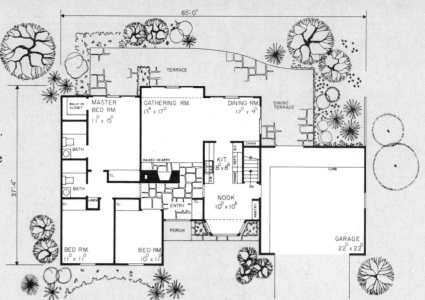

● This one-story traditionally styled design captures all the coziness and appeal of its more authentic 1½ and two-story counterparts. A study of the floor plans reveals a fine measure of livability. In less than 1,400 square feet, there are features galore. In addition to the two eating areas and the open planning of the gathering room, the indoor-outdoor relationships are of great interest. The basement may be developed for recreational activities. Blueprints for this design include two optional Contemporary exteriors. An excellent return on your construction dollars.

Design 152565

1,540 Sq. Ft.; 33,300 Cu. Ft.

● This modest sized floor plan has much to offer in the way of livability. It may function as either a two or three bedroom home. The family room is huge and features a fine, raised hearth fireplace. The open stairway to the basement is handy and will lead to what may be developed as the recreation area. In addition to the two full baths, there is an extra laundry room and the service entrance from the garage. The blueprints you receive for this design include details for building optional Tudor and Contemporary elevations. You'll have fun deciding upon your favorite.

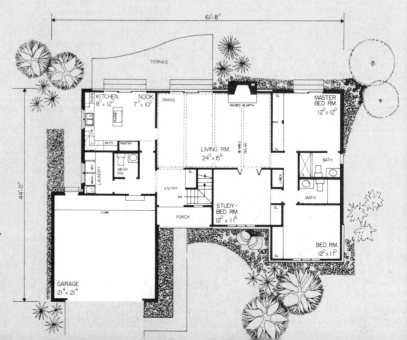

Design 152707
1,267 Sq. Ft.; 27,125 Cu. Ft.

● Here is a charming Early American adaptation that will serve as a picturesque and practical retirement home. Also, it will serve admirably those with a small family in search of an efficient, economically built home. The living area, highlighted by the raised hearth fireplace, is spacious. The kitchen features eating space; the bedroom area, two full baths. The dining room views the rear yard. Then, there is the basement for recreation and hobby pursuits. The bedroom wing offers three bedrooms and two full baths. Don't miss the sliding doors to terrace and the storage and pantry units.

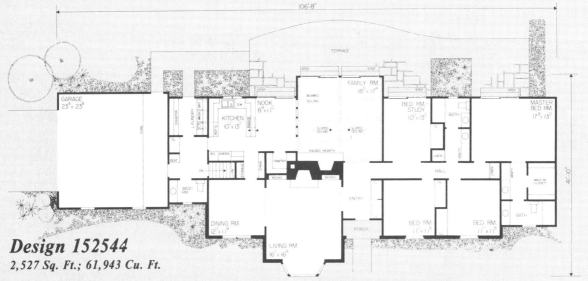

Design 152544

2,527 Sq. Ft.; 61,943 Cu. Ft.

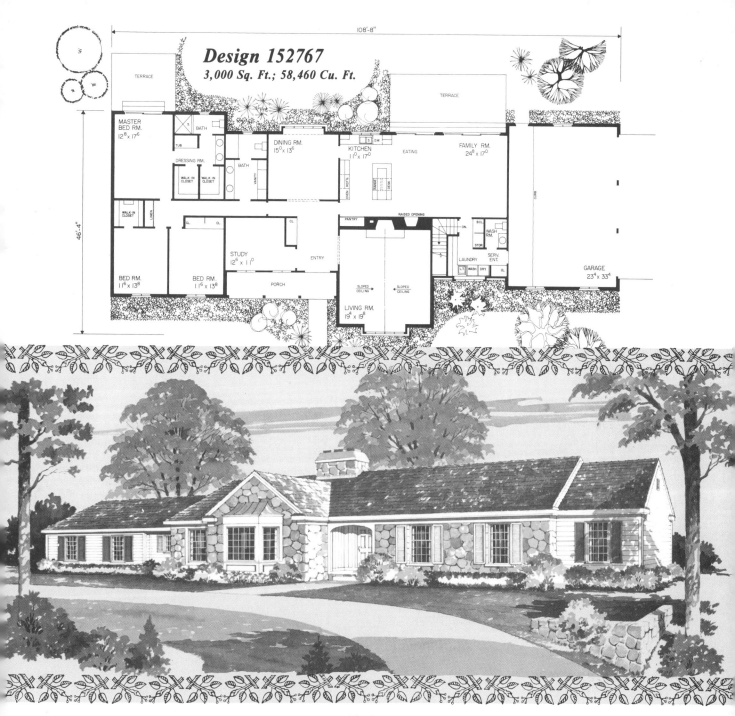

Design 152767
3,000 Sq. Ft.; 58,460 Cu. Ft.

108'-8"

46'-4"

TERRACE

TERRACE

MASTER BED RM. 12⁸ x 17⁶

BATH

TUB

DRESSING RM.

WALK IN CLOSET

WALK IN CLOSET

WALK IN CLOSET

LINEN

BED RM. 11⁶ x 13⁸

BED RM. 11⁶ x 13⁸

STUDY 12⁶ x 11⁰

ENTRY

PORCH

CL.

CL.

CL.

BATH

VANITY

DINING RM. 15⁰ x 13⁶

KITCHEN 11⁰ x 17⁰

EATING

OVEN REF'S.

RANGE

DESK

PANTRY

RAISED OPENING

LIVING RM. 19⁴ x 19⁸

SLOPED CEILING

SLOPED CEILING

FAMILY RM. 24⁸ x 17⁰

LAUNDRY

SERV. ENT.

WASH RM.

STOR.

L'T.

WASH

DRY.

GARAGE 23⁴ x 33⁴

Design 151761
2,548 Sq. Ft.; 43,870 Cu. Ft.

92'-10"

24'-0"   44'-0"   24'-0"

6'-0" 6'-0" 6'-0" 32'-0"

44'-10"

TERRACE

SHOP 11⁴ x 10⁰

BENCH

MUD RM.

W.

W.R.

L'T.

D.

CL.

B.C.

DN.

EATING

PASS-THRU

KIT. 21⁴ x 15⁶

FAMILY RM. 22⁴ x 15⁶

REF.G.

PN'TRY.

RANGE   BAR-B-Q

RAISED HEARTH

NICHE

DRESS. RM.

CL.

CL.

VANITY

BATH

BATH

VANITY

MASTER BED RM. 15⁴ x 13⁰

BED RM. 11⁶ x 12⁰

GARAGE 23⁴ x 21⁰

DINING RM. 12⁰ x 13⁶

LIVING RM. 23⁴ x 13⁶

ENTRANCE COURT

ENTRY HALL

CL.

CL.

LIN.

CL.

CL.

BED RM. 11⁶ x 12⁰

BED RM. 11⁶ x 15⁴

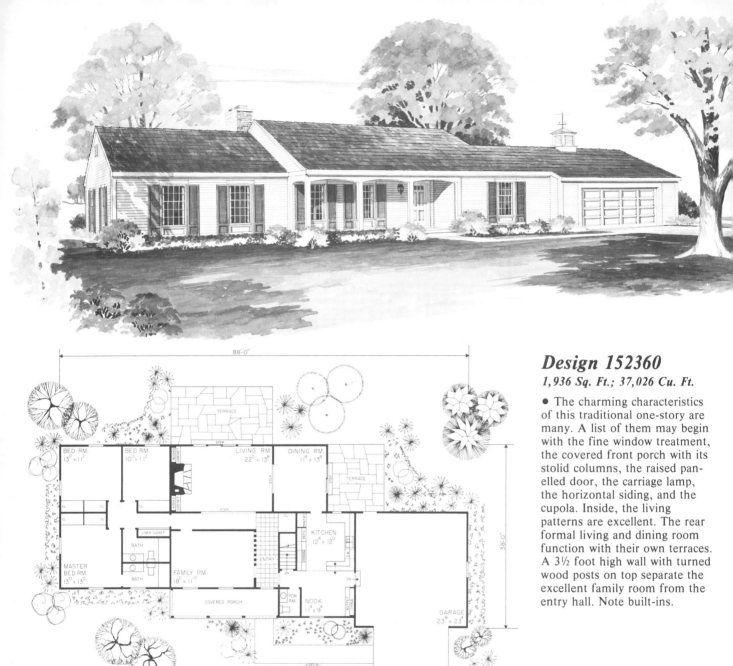

Design 152360
1,936 Sq. Ft.; 37,026 Cu. Ft.

● The charming characteristics of this traditional one-story are many. A list of them may begin with the fine window treatment, the covered front porch with its stolid columns, the raised panelled door, the carriage lamp, the horizontal siding, and the cupola. Inside, the living patterns are excellent. The rear formal living and dining room function with their own terraces. A 3½ foot high wall with turned wood posts on top separate the excellent family room from the entry hall. Note built-ins.

Design 152597
1,515 Sq. Ft.; 32,000 Cu. Ft.

● Whether it be a starter house you are after, or one in which to spend your retirement years, this pleasing frame home will provide a full measure of pride of ownership. It functions in an orderly and efficient manner. The 26 foot gathering room will even take care of those formal dining occasions. There are two full baths, plenty of storage facilities, two sets of sliding glass doors to the terraces, a fireplace, basement, and an attached two-car garage.

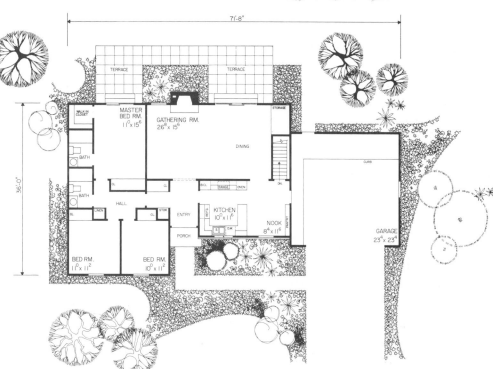

Design 151929
2,312 Sq. Ft.; 26,364 Cu. Ft.

● This home will lead the hit parade in your new subdivision. Its sparkling, traditionally styled exterior will be the favorite of all that pass. And, once inside, friends will marvel at how the plan just seems to cater to your family's every activity. For formal entertaining, there is the sunken living room and the separate dining room. For in-formal livability, there's the beamed ceilinged family room and the outdoor terrace.

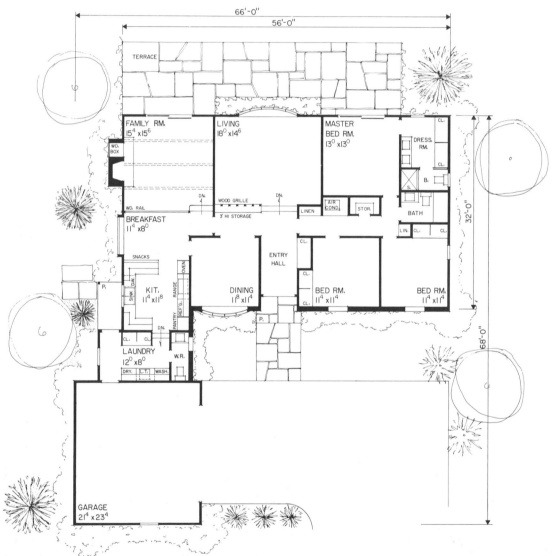

Design 151949 *1,992 Sq. Ft.; 23,764 Cu. Ft.*

● Surely a prize winner. Whether the contest be to pick the best in exterior appeal, or the finest in true livability, this L-shaped home will score at the top. The curving drive is a charming approach to the inviting front doors of the center entrance. The tra-

ditionally styled windows, the cupola, the contrasting siding materials of masonry and wood (or make it aluminum, if you prefer), the interesting roof lines, and the excellent proportions, are the exterior features which catch the eye. Inside, the highlights are,

indeed, numerous. Of particular interest are the family and living rooms. Both are sunken to a depth of two steps, are free from traffic and are looking out upon the rear yard. That is a beamed ceiling in family room. Don't miss the wood box.

● A sizeable master bedroom with a dressing area featuring two walk-in closets, a twin lavatory, and compartmented bath. A two-bedroom children's area with full bath and supporting study. A formal living and dining zone separated by a thru-fireplace. A spacious kitchen-nook with a cheerfully informal sun room just a step away through sliding glass doors. A service area with laundry, storage, wash room and stairs to basement. An array of sliding glass doors leading to outdoor living on the various functional terraces. These are but some of the highlights of this appealing traditional.

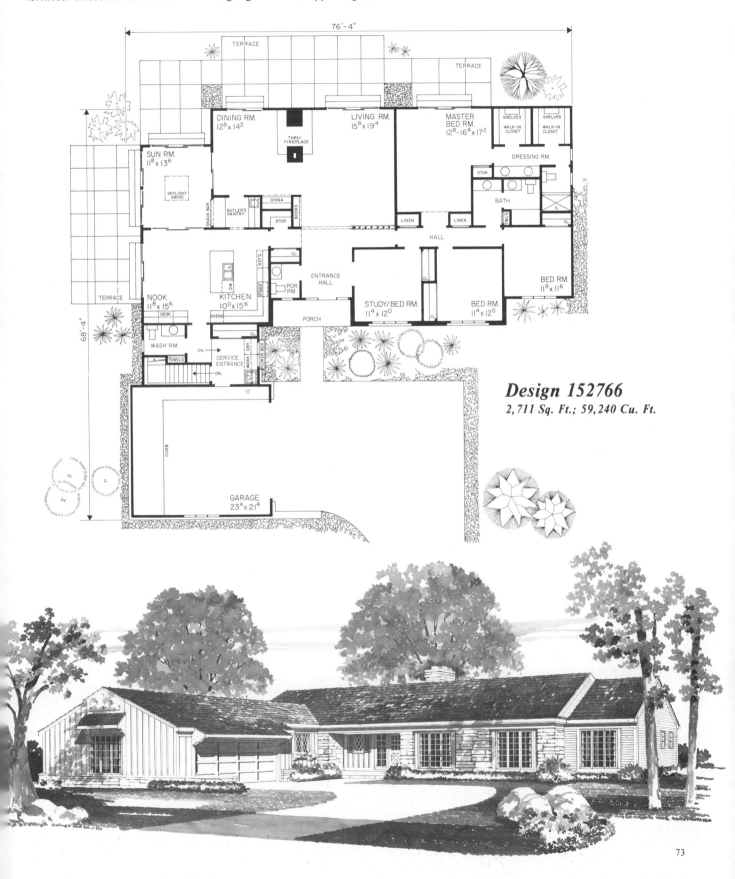

Design 152766
2,711 Sq. Ft.; 59,240 Cu. Ft.

Design 151939
1,387 Sq. Ft.; 28,000 Cu. Ft.

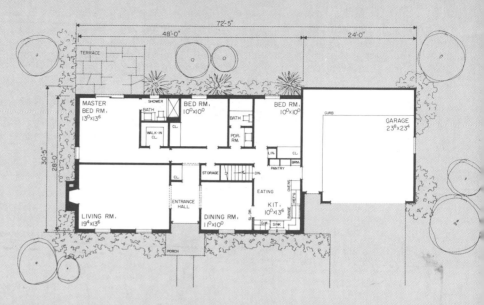

● A delightfully proportioned house with more than its full share of charm. The brick veneer exterior contrasts pleasingly with the narrow horizontal siding of the oversized attached two-car garage. Perhaps the focal point of the exterior is the recessed front entrance with its double colonial styled doors. The secondary, service entrance through the garage to the kitchen area is a handy feature. The pantry units are strategically located as are the stairs to the basement. The efficient, L-shaped kitchen highlights extra space for eating.

Design 151346
1,644 Sq. Ft.; 19,070 Cu. Ft.

● Whether you enter through the service door of the attached garage, or through the centered front entry your appreciation of what this plan has to offer will grow. The mud room area is certainly an outstanding feature. Traffic flows from this area to the informal family room with its fireplace and access to the rear terrace.

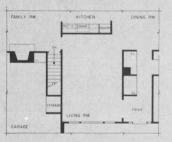

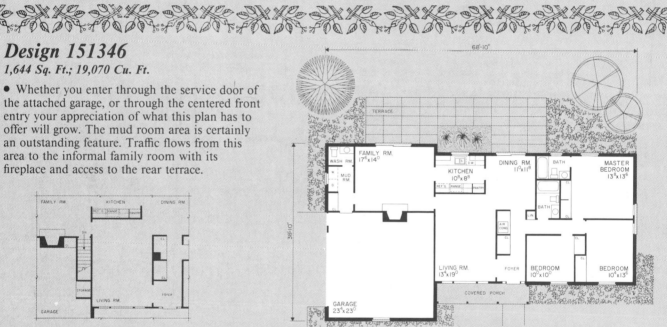

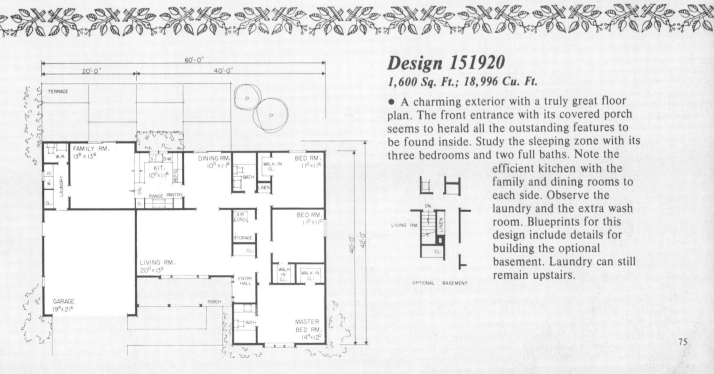

OPTIONAL BASEMENT

Design 151920

1,600 Sq. Ft.; 18,996 Cu. Ft.

● A charming exterior with a truly great floor plan. The front entrance with its covered porch seems to herald all the outstanding features to be found inside. Study the sleeping zone with its three bedrooms and two full baths. Note the efficient kitchen with the family and dining rooms to each side. Observe the laundry and the extra wash room. Blueprints for this design include details for building the optional basement. Laundry can still remain upstairs.

Design 151829
1,800 Sq. Ft.; 32,236 Cu. Ft.

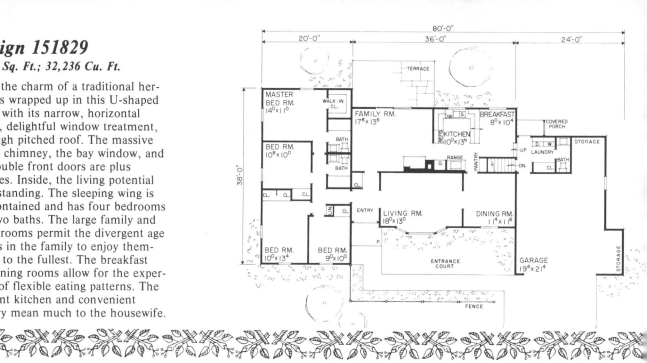

● All the charm of a traditional heritage is wrapped up in this U-shaped home with its narrow, horizontal siding, delightful window treatment, and high pitched roof. The massive center chimney, the bay window, and the double front doors are plus features. Inside, the living potential is outstanding. The sleeping wing is self-contained and has four bedrooms and two baths. The large family and living rooms permit the divergent age groups in the family to enjoy themselves to the fullest. The breakfast and dining rooms allow for the experience of flexible eating patterns. The efficient kitchen and convenient laundry mean much to the housewife.

Design 151980
1,901 Sq. Ft.; 36,240 Cu. Ft.

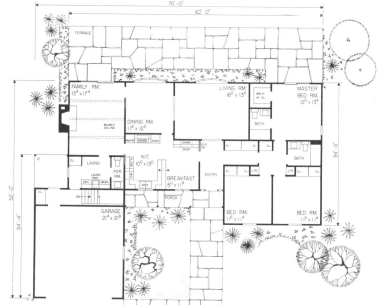

● Planned for easy living, the livability patterns of the active family will be pleasant ones, indeed. All the elements are present to assure a wonderful family life. The impressive exterior is enhanced by the recessed front entrance area with its covered porch. The center entry results in a convenient and efficient flow of traffic. A secondary entrance leads from the covered side porch, or the garage, into the first floor laundry. Note the powder room nearby. Imagine, each of the three main living areas - the family, dining and living rooms - look out upon the rear yard.

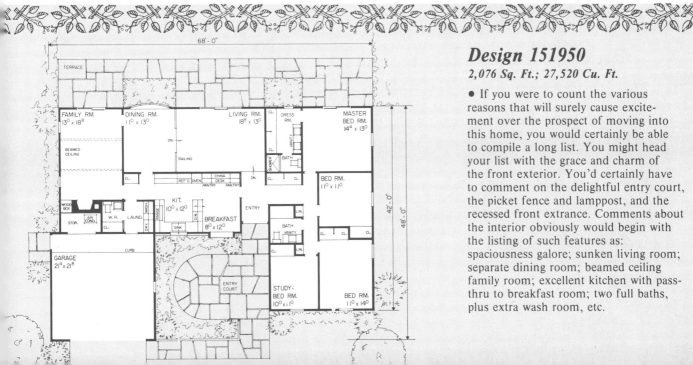

Design 151950
2,076 Sq. Ft.; 27,520 Cu. Ft.

● If you were to count the various reasons that will surely cause excitement over the prospect of moving into this home, you would certainly be able to compile a long list. You might head your list with the grace and charm of the front exterior. You'd certainly have to comment on the delightful entry court, the picket fence and lamppost, and the recessed front extrance. Comments about the interior obviously would begin with the listing of such features as: spaciousness galore; sunken living room; separate dining room; beamed ceiling family room; excellent kitchen with pass-thru to breakfast room; two full baths, plus extra wash room, etc.

77

Design 152739
3,313 Sq. Ft.; 65,230 Cu. Ft.

● What an impressive rambling one-story home this is. Its Early American flavor is captured by the effective window and door treatment, the cornice-work, and the stolid porch pillars. The interior leaves nothing to be desired. There are three bedrooms and two full baths in sleeping area. The living zone facilities are spacious. The kitchen/laundry area is outstanding. Then, there is extra guest room. A live-in relative would enjoy the privacy of this room. Full bath is nearby.

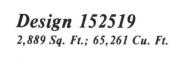

Design 152519
2,889 Sq. Ft.; 65,261 Cu. Ft.

● What a pleasing, traditional exterior. And what a fine, convenient living interior! The configuration of this home leads to interesting roof planes and even functional outdoor terrace areas. The front court and the covered porch strike an enchanting note. The gathering room will be just that. It will be the family's multi-purpose living area. Just adjacent to the foyer is the open stairwell to basement level and the recreation area.

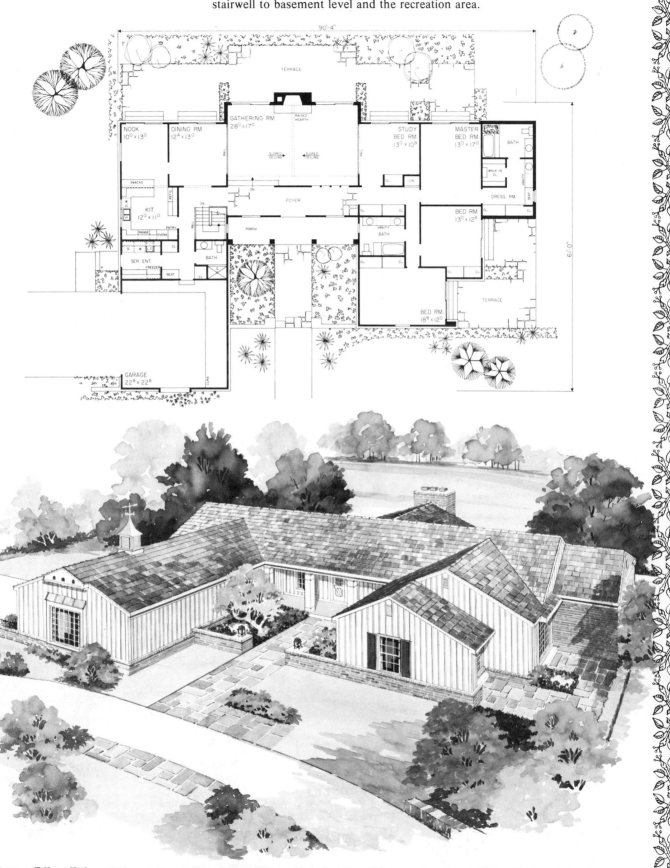

Design 152181

2,612 Sq. Ft.
45,230 Cu. Ft.

● Here is a rambling traditionally styled ranch home that differs only slightly from its counterpart on the opposing page. It is slightly larger in size and, of course, has its floor plan reversed from left to right. It is hard to imagine a home with any more eye-appeal than this one. It is the complete picture of charm. The interior is no less outstanding. Sliding glass doors permit the large master bedroom, the quiet living room, and the all-purpose family room to function directly with the outdoors.

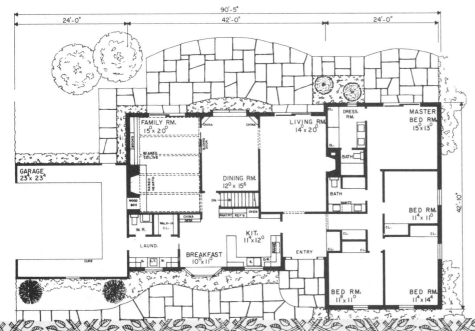

Design 152144
2,432 Sq. Ft.; 42,519 Cu. Ft.

● Have you ever wished you lived in a house in which the living, dining, and family rooms all looked out upon the rear terrace? Further, have you ever wished your home had its kitchen located to the front so that you could see approaching callers? Or, have you ever wished for a house where traffic in from the garage was stopped right in the laundry so that wet, snowy, dirty, and muddy apparel could be shed immediately? Of course, you've probably wished many times for a quiet four bedroom, two bath sleeping zone.

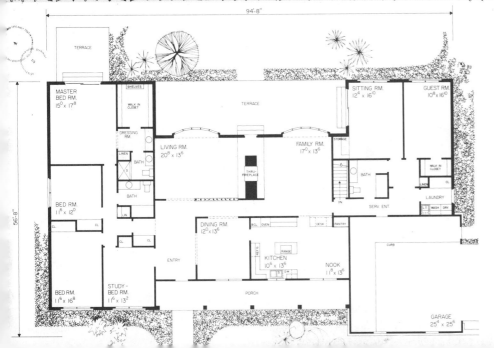

Design 152768
3,436 Sq. Ft.; 65,450 Cu. Ft.

● Besides its elegant traditionally styled exterior with its delightfully long covered front porch, this home has an exceptionally livable interior. There is the outstanding four-bedroom, two-bath sleeping wing. Then, the efficient front kitchen flanked by the formal and informal dining areas. Separated by the two-way, thru fireplace are the living and family rooms which look out on the rear yard. Worthy of particular note is the development of a potential live-in relative facility. These two rooms would also serve the large family well as a hobby room and library.

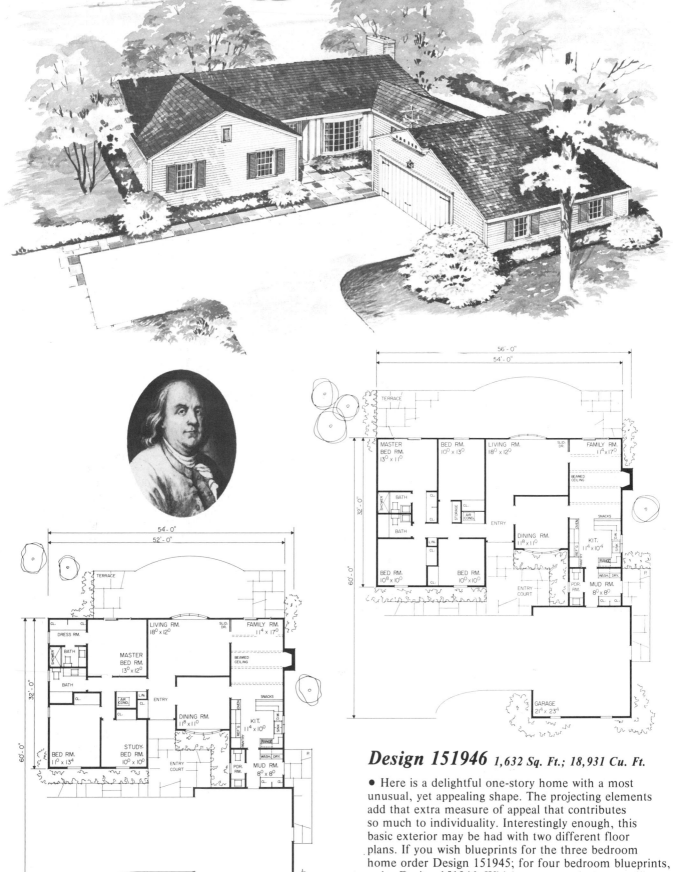

Design 151945
1,568 Sq. Ft.; 18,188 Cu. Ft.

Design 151946 *1,632 Sq. Ft.; 18,931 Cu. Ft.*

● Here is a delightful one-story home with a most unusual, yet appealing shape. The projecting elements add that extra measure of appeal that contributes so much to individuality. Interestingly enough, this basic exterior may be had with two different floor plans. If you wish blueprints for the three bedroom home order Design 151945; for four bedroom blueprints, order Design 151946. Whichever you select, you will enjoy the efficiency of the remainder of the plan. There are formal living and dining rooms, an informal beamed ceilinged family room, a fine U-shaped kitchen, and a strategically placed mud room with an adjacent powder room.

Multi-Level Homes

Design 151705

896 Sq. Ft. - Main Level
870 Sq. Ft. - Lower Level
896 Sq. Ft. - Upper Level
27,040 Cu. Ft.

BED RM.
10⁰ x 10⁰ — 10' x 10'

BATH

MASTER BED RM.
15⁴ x 13⁶ — 15'4" x 13'6"

WALK IN CL.

LINEN

CL.

DN.

CL.

CL.

BED RM.
11⁰ x 10⁰ — 11' x 10'

BATH

VANITY

BED RM.
11⁸ x 11⁴ — 11'8" x 11'4"

● A gently sloping, suburban site will be just the location for this superb traditional tri-level home. The main level has both a formal living room and a separate dining room. In addition, there is the informal eating area of the kitchen. The lower level features a fine family room with snack bar, raised hearth fireplace and glass sliding doors to the lower terrace. There are also two well-lighted rooms which may function as additional bedrooms. Don't miss the full bath and the laundry area. A covered porch with a built-in barbecue unit attaches house and two-car garage. There are four bedrooms on the upper level.

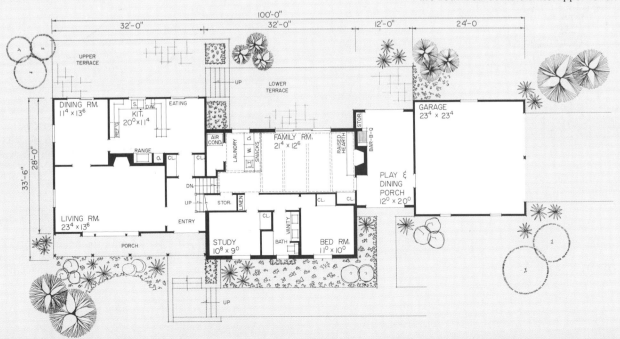

100'-0"

32'-0"   32'-0"   12'-0"   24'-0

28'-0"

33'-6"

UPPER TERRACE

LOWER TERRACE

UP

DINING RM.
11⁴ x 13⁶

EATING

KIT.
20⁰ x 11⁴

REFG

RANGE

O.

CL.

CL.

AIR COND.

LAUNDRY

W. D.

SNACKS

FAMILY RM.
21⁴ x 12⁶

RAISED HEARTH

STOR.

BAR-B-Q

GARAGE
23⁴ x 23⁴

DN.

UP

STOR.

LINEN

CL.

VANITY

BATH

CL.

CL.

PLAY & DINING PORCH
12⁰ x 20⁰

LIVING RM.
23⁴ x 13⁶

ENTRY

PORCH

STUDY
10⁸ x 9⁰

BED RM.
11⁰ x 10⁰

UP

Design 151977 *896 Sq. Ft. - Main Level; 884 Sq. Ft. - Upper Level; 896 Sq. Ft. - Lower Level; 36, 718 Cu. Ft.*

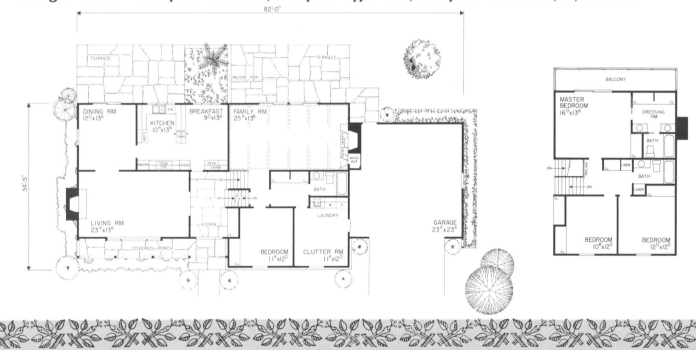

Design 152216

1,183 Sq. Ft. - Main Level; 1,344 Sq. Ft. - Upper Level
659 Sq. Ft. - Lower Level; 51,856 Cu. Ft.

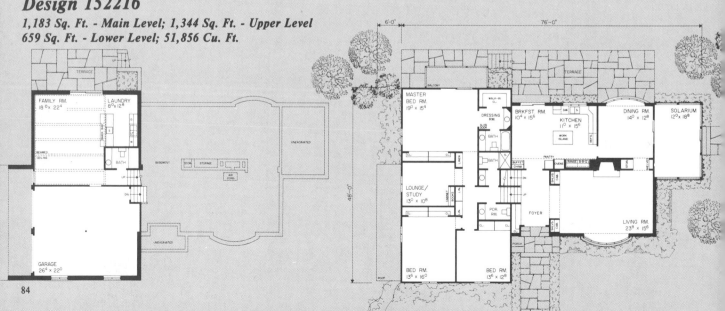

Design 152125 728 Sq. Ft. - Main Level; 672 Sq. Ft. - Upper Level; 656 Sq. Ft. - Lower Level; 28,315 Cu. Ft.

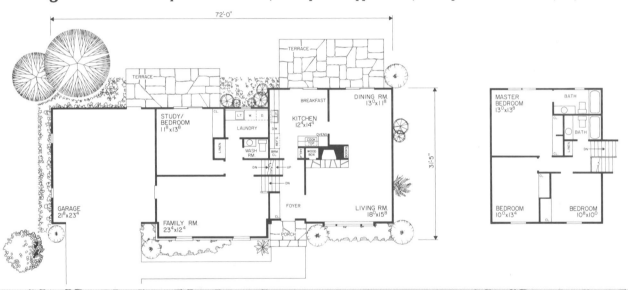

Design 151935 *904 Sq. Ft. - Main Level; 864 Sq. Ft. - Upper Level; 840 Sq. Ft. - Lower Level; 26,745 Cu. Ft.*

Design 151927 *1,272 Sq. Ft. - Main Level; 960 Sq. Ft. - Upper Level; 936 Sq. Ft. - Lower Level; 36,815 Cu. Ft.*

Design 152727

506 Sq. Ft. - Entry Level; 1,241 Sq. Ft. - Lower Level
1,288 Sq. Ft. - Upper Level; 38,590 Cu. Ft.

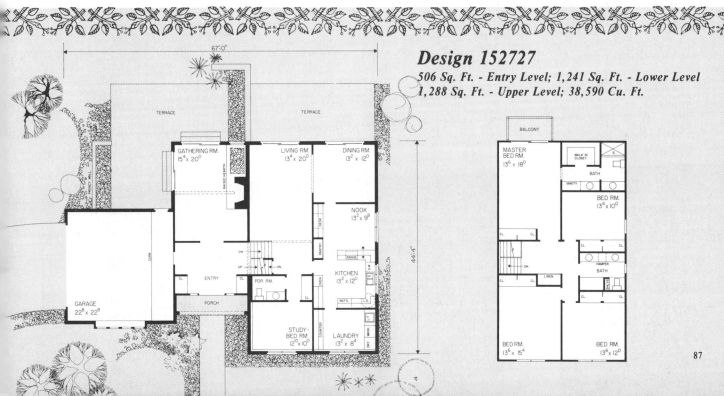

Design 151358

576 Sq. Ft. - Main Level
672 Sq. Ft. - Upper Level
328 Sq. Ft. - Lower Level
20,784 Cu. Ft.

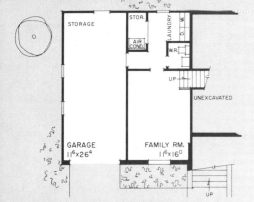

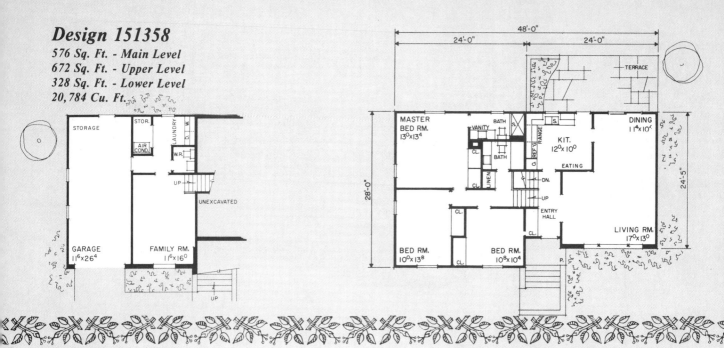

Design 151981

784 Sq. Ft. - Main Level; 912 Sq. Ft. - Upper Level
336 Sq. Ft. - Lower Level; 26,618 Cu. Ft.

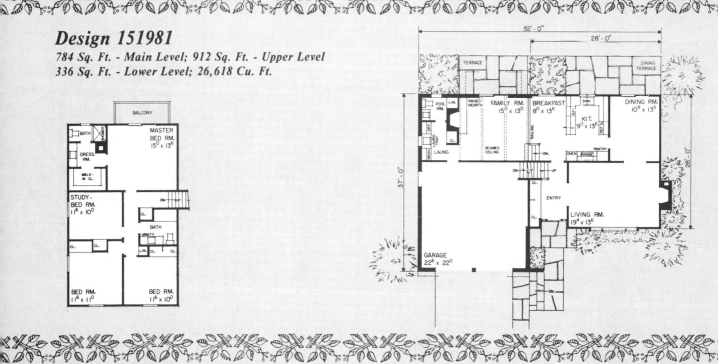

Design 151308

496 Sq. Ft. - Main Level
572 Sq. Ft. - Upper Level
537 Sq. Ft. - Lower Level
16,024 Cu. Ft.

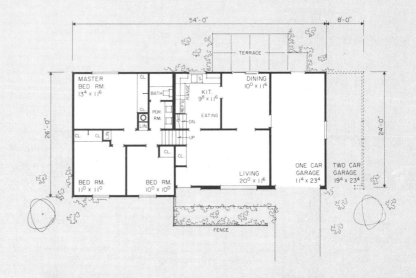

89

Design 151985

884 Sq. Ft. - Main Level; 960 Sq. Ft. - Upper Level
888 Sq. Ft. - Lower Level; 29,743 Cu. Ft.

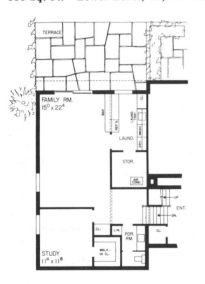

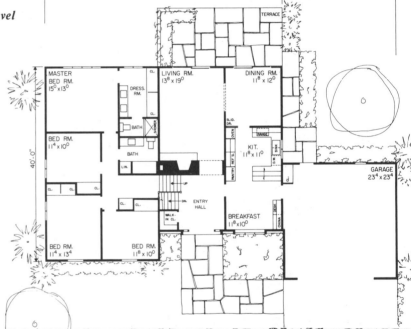

Design 152514

1,713 Sq. Ft. - Upper Level
916 Sq. Ft. - Lower Level
32,000 Cu. Ft.

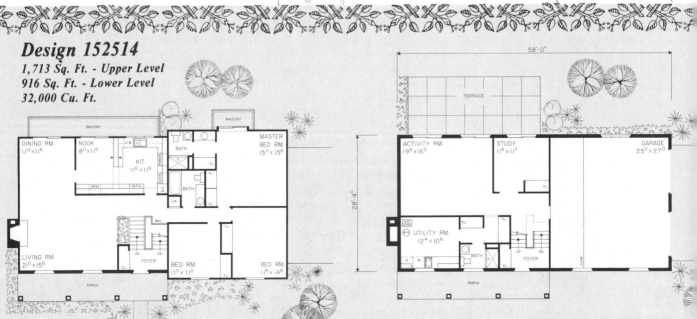

Design 151768 *844 Sq. Ft. - Main Level; 740 Sq. Ft. - Upper Level; 740 Sq. Ft. - Lower Level; 29,455 Cu. Ft.*

● Here are three traditionally styled exteriors each of which house varying patterns of livability. Design 151985, at left, is a tri-level with four bedrooms, a spacious living level, and a study plus family room on the lower level. Design 151768 is a quad-level with three bedrooms and an extra basement level. Design 152514 is a split foyer type bi-level. It has its major livability on the upper level with bright and cheerful bonus space below. Which design suits your family's living patterns best?

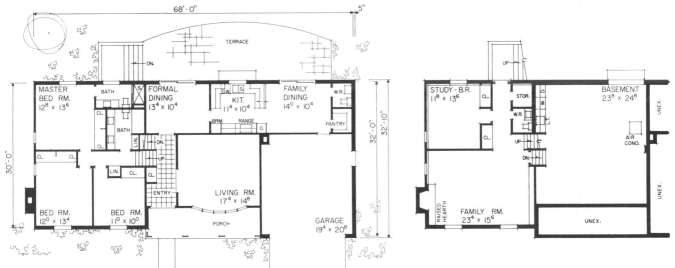

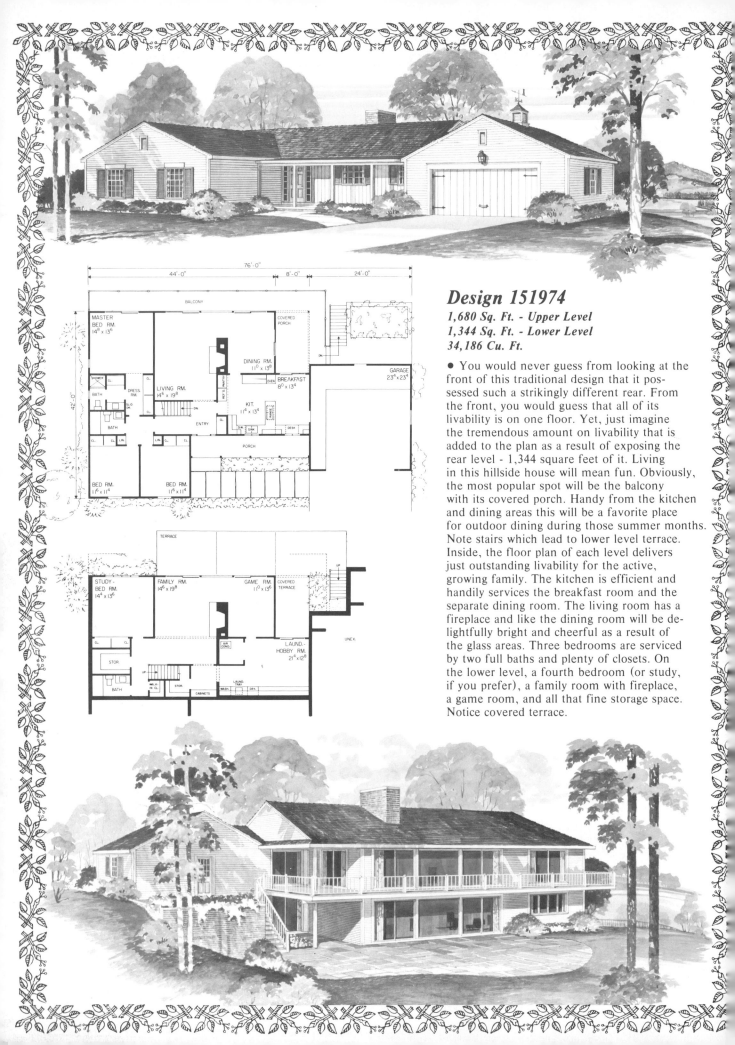

Design 151974

1,680 Sq. Ft. - Upper Level
1,344 Sq. Ft. - Lower Level
34,186 Cu. Ft.

● You would never guess from looking at the front of this traditional design that it possessed such a strikingly different rear. From the front, you would guess that all of its livability is on one floor. Yet, just imagine the tremendous amount on livability that is added to the plan as a result of exposing the rear level - 1,344 square feet of it. Living in this hillside house will mean fun. Obviously, the most popular spot will be the balcony with its covered porch. Handy from the kitchen and dining areas this will be a favorite place for outdoor dining during those summer months. Note stairs which lead to lower level terrace. Inside, the floor plan of each level delivers just outstanding livability for the active, growing family. The kitchen is efficient and handily services the breakfast room and the separate dining room. The living room has a fireplace and like the dining room will be delightfully bright and cheerful as a result of the glass areas. Three bedrooms are serviced by two full baths and plenty of closets. On the lower level, a fourth bedroom (or study, if you prefer), a family room with fireplace, a game room, and all that fine storage space. Notice covered terrace.

All The "TOOLS" You And Your Builder Need. . .

1. THE PLAN BOOKS

Home Planners' unique Design Category Series makes it easy to look at and study only the types of designs for which you and your family have an interest. Each of six plan books features a specific type of home, namely: Two-Story, 1½ Story, One-Story Over 2000 Sq. Ft., One-Story Under 2000 Sq. Ft., Multi-Levels and Vacation Homes. In addition to the convenient Design Category Series, there is an impressive selection of other current titles. While the home plans featured in these books are also to be found in the Design Category Series, they, too, are edited for those with special tastes and requirements. Your family will spend many enjoyable hours reviewing the delightfully designed exteriors and the practical floor plans. Surely your home or office library should include a selection of these popular plan books. Your complete satisfaction is guaranteed.

2. THE CONSTRUCTION BLUEPRINTS

There are blueprints available for each of the designs published in Home Planners' current plan books. Depending upon the size, the style and the type of home, each set of blueprints consists of from five to ten large sheets. Only by studying the blueprints is it possible to give complete and final consideration to the proper selection of a design for your next home. The blueprints provide the opportunity for all family members to familiarize themselves with the features of all exterior elevations, interior elevations and details, all dimensions, special built-in features and effects. They also provide a full understanding of the materials to be used and/or selected. The low-cost of our blueprints makes it possible and indeed, practical, to study in detail a number of different sets of blueprints before deciding upon which design to build.

3. THE MATERIALS LIST

A separate list of materials, available for a small fee, is an important part of the plan package. It comprises the last sheet of each set of blueprints and serves as a handy reference during the period of construction. Of course, at the pricing and the material ordering stages, it is indispensable.

4. THE SPECIFICATION OUTLINE

Each order for blueprints is accompanied by one Specification Outline. You and your builder will find this a time-saving tool when deciding upon your own individual specifications. An important reference document should you wish to write your own specifications.

5. THE PLUMBING & ELECTRICAL PACKAGE

The construction blueprints you order from Home Planners, Inc. include locations for all plumbing fixtures — sinks, lavatories, tubs, showers, water closets, laundry trays, hot water heaters, etc. The blueprints also show the locations of all electrical switches, plugs, and outlets. These plumbing and electrical details are sufficient to present to your local contractor for discussions about your individual specifications and subsequent installations in conformance with local codes. However, for those who wish to acquaint themselves with many of the intricacies of residential plumbing and electrical details and installations, Home Planners, Inc. has made available this package. We do not recommend that the layman attempt to do his own plumbing and electrical work. It is, nevertheless, advisable that owners be as knowledgeable as possible about each of these disciplines. The entire family will appreciate the educational value of these low-cost, easy-to-understand details.

The Design Category Series

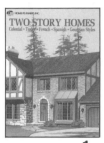

360 TWO STORY HOMES

English Tudors, Early American Salt Boxes, Gambrels, Farmhouses, Southern Colonials, Georgians, French Mansards, Contemporaries. Interesting floor plans for both small and large families. Efficient kitchens, 2 to 6 bedrooms, family rooms, libraries, extra baths, mud rooms. Homes for all budgets.

1. 288 Pages, $6.95

150 1½ STORY HOMES

Cape Cod, Williamsburg, Georgian, Tudor and Contemporary versions. Low budget and country-estate feature sections. Expandable family plans. Formal and informal living and dining areas along with gathering rooms. Spacious, country kitchens. Indoor-outdoor livability with covered porches and functional terraces.

2. 128 Pages, $3.95

210 ONE STORY HOMES OVER 2,000 Sq. Ft.

All popular styles. Including Spanish, Western, Tudor French, and other traditional versions. Contemporaries. Gracious, family living patterns. Sunken living rooms, master bedroom suites, atriums, courtyards, pools. Fine indoor-outdoor living relationships. For modest to country-estate budgets.

3. 192 Pages, $4.95

315 ONE STORY HOMES UNDER 2,000 Sq. Ft.

A great selection of traditional and contemporary exteriors for medium and restricted budgets. Efficient, practical floor plans. Gathering rooms, formal and informal living and dining rooms, mud rooms, indoor-outdoor livability. Economically built homes. Designs with bonus space livability for growing families.

4. 192 Pages, $4.95

215 MULTI-LEVEL HOMES

For new dimensions in family living. A captivating variety of exterior styles, exciting floor plans for flat and sloping sites. Exposed lower levels. Balconies, decks. Plans for the active family. Upper level lounges, excellent bath facilities. Sloping ceilings. Functional outdoor terraces. For all building budgets.

5. 192 Pages, $4.95

223 VACATION HOMES

Features A-Frames, Chalets, Hexagons, economical rectangles. One and two stories plus multi-levels. Lodges for year 'round livability. From 480 to 3238 sq. ft. Cottages sleeping 4 to 22. For flat or sloping sites. Spacious, open planning. Over 600 illustrations. 120 Pages in full color. Cluster home selection. For lakeshore or woodland leisure living.

6. 176 Pages, $4.95

The Exterior Style Series

330 EARLY AMERICAN HOME PLANS

Our new *Essential Guide to Early American Home Plans* traces Early American architecture from our Colonial Past to Traditional styles popular today with a written history of designs and colorful sections devoted to styles. Many of our designs are patterned after historic homes.

7. 304 Pages, $9.95

335 CONTEMPORARY HOME PLANS

Our new *Essential Guide to Contemporary Home Plans* offers a colorful directory to modern architecture, including a history of American Contemporary styling and more than 335 home plans of all sizes and popular designs. 304 colorful pages! Must reading.

8. 304 Pages, $9.95

135 ENGLISH TUDOR HOMES

and other Popular Family Plans is a favorite of many. The current popularity of the English Tudor home design is phenomenal. Here is a book which is loaded with Tudors for all budgets. There are one-story, 1½ and two-story designs, plus multi-levels and hillsides from 1,176–3,849 sq. ft.

9. 104 Pages, $3.95

The Budget Series

175 LOW BUDGET HOMES

A special selection of home designs for the modest or restricted building budget. An excellent variety of Traditional and Contemporary designs. One-story, 1½ and two-story and split-level homes. Three, four and five bedrooms. Family rooms, extra baths, formal and informal dining rooms. Basement and non-basement designs. Attached garages and covered porches.

11. 96 Pages, $2.95

165 AFFORDABLE HOME PLANS

This outstanding book was specially edited with a wide selection of houses and plans for those with a medium building budget. While none of these designs are considered low-cost; neither do they require an unlimited budget to build. Square footages range from 1,428. Exteriors of Tudor, French, Early American, Spanish and Contemporary are included.

12. 112 Pages, $2.95

142 HOME DESIGNS FOR EXPANDED BUILDING BUDGETS

A family's ability to finance and need for a larger home grows as its size and income increases. This selection highlights designs which house an average square footage of 2,551. One-story plans average 2,069; two-stories, 2,738; multi-levels, 2,825. Spacious homes featuring raised hearth fireplaces, open planning and efficient kitchens.

13. 112 Pages, $2.95

General Interest Titles

ENCYCLOPEDIA - 450 PLANS

For those who wish to review and study perhaps the largest selection of designs available in a single volume. Varying exterior styles, plus interesting and practical floor plans for all building budgets. Formal, informal living patterns; indoor-outdoor livability; small, growing and large family facilities.

15.

320 Pages, $9.95

244 HOUSE PLANS FOR BETTER LIVING

Special 40th Anniversary Edition with over 650 illustrations. Sectionalized to highlight special interest groups of designs. A fine introduction to our special interest titles. All styles, sizes, and types of homes are represented. Designs feature gathering rooms, country kitchens, second-floor lounges.

16.

192 Pages $3.50

HOME PLANS FOR OUTDOOR LIVING

This superbly produced, 192-page volume showcases more than 100 home designs, each uniquely styled to bring the outdoors in. Terraces. Decks. Porches. Balconies. Courtyards. Atriums. Sunspaces. All have a place in the book, with livable home plans designed to bring the ideas down to earth and put them to work.

17.

192 Pages, $10.95

COLOR PORTFOLIO – 310 DESIGNS

An expanded full-color guide to our most popular Early American, Spanish, French, Tudor, Contemporary, and modern Trend home designs. 310 home plans of all popular styles and sizes. Includes energy-efficient designs. Plans for varying building budgets. One, 1½, two-story, and split-level designs for all terrain. This is our largest full-color book with our newest trend-setting designs and other favorites. It's must reading for the serious home planner.

18.

288 Pages in Full Color, $12.95

136 SPANISH & WESTERN HOME DESIGNS

Stucco exteriors, arches, tile roofs, wide-overhangs, courtyards and rambling ranches are characteristics which make this design selection distinctive. These sun-country designs highlight indoor-outdoor relationships. Solar oriented livability is featured.

10. **120 Pages, $3.95**

PLAN BOOKS are a valuable tool for anyone who plans to build a new home. After you have selected a home design that satisifies your list of requirements, you can order blueprints for further study.

115 HOME DESIGNS FOR UNLIMITED BUILDING BUDGETS

This book will appeal to those with large families and the desire and wherewithal to satisfy all the family needs, plus most of their wants. The upscale designs in this portfolio average 3,132 square feet. One-story designs average 2,796 sq. ft.; 1½-story, 3,188 sq. ft.; two-story, 3,477 sq. ft.; multi-level, 3,532 sq. ft. Truly designs for elegant living.

14.

112 Pages, $2.95

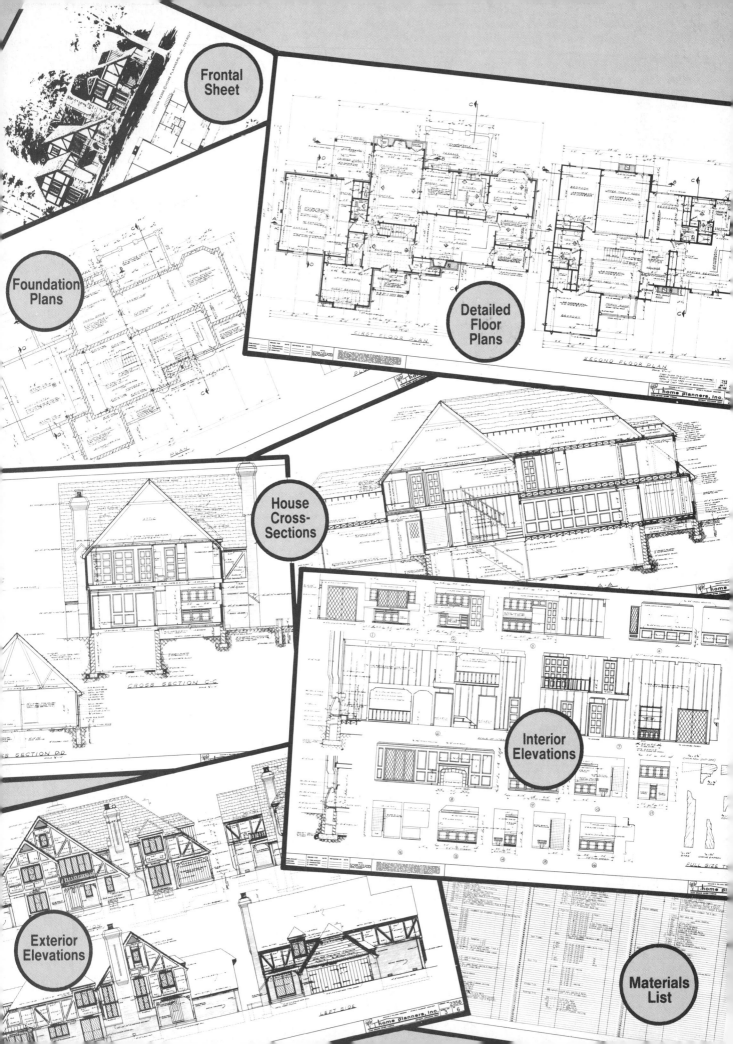

Frontal
Sheet

Foundation
Plans

Detailed
Floor
Plans

House
Cross-
Sections

Interior
Elevations

Exterior
Elevations

Materials
List

The Blueprints

1. FRONTAL SHEET.
Artist's landscaped sketch of the exterior and ink-line floor plans are on the frontal sheet of each set of blueprints.

2. FOUNDATION PLAN.
¼" Scale basement and foundation plan. All necessary notations and dimensions. Plot plan diagram for locating house on building site.

3. DETAILED FLOOR PLAN.
¼" Scale first and second floor plans with complete dimensions. Cross-section detail keys. Diagrammatic layout of electrical outlets and switches.

4. HOUSE CROSS-SECTIONS.
Large scale sections of foundation, interior and exterior walls, floors and roof details for design and construction control.

5. INTERIOR ELEVATIONS.
Large scale interior details of the complete kitchen cabinet design, bathrooms, powder room, laundry, fireplaces, paneling, beam ceilings, built-in cabinets, etc.

6. EXTERIOR ELEVATIONS.
¼" Scale exterior elevation drawings of front, rear, and both sides of the house. All exterior materials and details are shown to indicate the complete design and proportions of the house.

7. MATERIALS LIST.
For a small additional fee, complete lists of all materials required for the construction of the house as designed are included in each set of blueprints (one charge for any size order).

THIS BLUEPRINT PACKAGE
will help you and your family take a major step forward in the final appraisal and planning of your new home. Only by spending many enjoyable and informative hours studying the numerous details included in the complete package will you feel sure of, and comfortable with, your commitment to build your new home. To assure successful and productive consultation with your builder and/or architect, reference to the various elements of the blueprint package is a must. The blueprints, materials list and specification outline will save much consultation time and expense. Don't be without them.

The Materials List

For a small extra charge, you will receive a materials list with each set of blueprints you order (one fee for any size order). Each list shows you the quantity, type and size of the non-mechanical materials required to build your home. It also tells you where these materials are used. This makes the blueprints easy to understand.

Influencing the mechanical requirements are geographical differences in availability of materials, local codes, methods of installation and individual preferences. Because of these factors, your local heating, plumbing and electrical contractors can supply you with necessary material take-offs for their particular trades.

Materials lists simplify your material ordering and enable you to get quicker price quotations from your builder and material dealer. Because the materials list is an integral part of each set of blueprints, it is not available separately.

Among the materials listed:

• Masonry, Veneer & Fireplace • Framing Lumber • Roofing & Sheet Metal • Windows & Door Frames • Exterior Trim & Insulation • Tile Work, Finish Floors • Interior Trim, Kitchen Cabinets • Rough & Finish Hardware

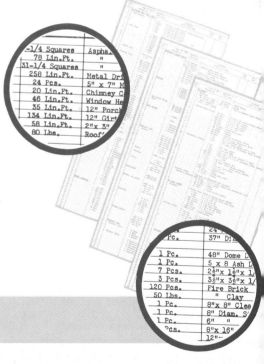

The Specification Outline

This fill-in type specification lists over 150 phases of home construction from excavating to painting and includes wiring, plumbing, heating and air-conditioning. It consists of 16 pages and will prove invaluable for specifying to your builder the exact materials, equipment and methods of construction you want in your new home. One Specification Outline is included free with each order for blueprints. Additional Specification Outlines are available at $3.00 each.

CONTENTS
• General Instructions, Suggestions and Information • Excavating and Grading • Masonry and Concrete Work • Sheet Metal Work • Carpentry, Millwork, Roofing, and Miscellaneous Items • Lath and Plaster or Drywall Wallboard • Schedule for Room Finishes • Painting and Finishing • Tile Work • Electrical Work • Plumbing • Heating and Air-Conditioning

Before You Order

1. STUDY THE DESIGNS . . . found in Home Planners books. As you review these delightful custom homes, you should keep in mind the total living requirements of your family — both indoors and outdoors. Although we do not make changes in plans, many minor changes can be made prior to the period of construction. If major changes are involved to satisfy your personal requirements, you should consider ordering one set of blueprints and having them redrawn locally. Consultation with your architect is strongly advised when contemplating major changes.

2. HOW TO ORDER BLUEPRINTS . . . After you have chosen the design that satisfies your requirements, or if you have selected one that you wish to study in more detail, simply clip the accompanying order blank and mail with your remittance. However, if it is not convenient for you to send a check or money order, you can use your credit card, or merely indicate C.O.D. shipment. Postman will collect all charges, including postage and C.O.D. fee. C.O.D. shipments are not permitted to Canada or foreign countries. Should time be of essence, as it sometimes is with many of our customers, your telephone order usually can be processed and shipped in the next day's mail. Simply call toll free 1-800-521-6797, (Michigan residents call collect 0-313-477-1850).

3. OUR SERVICE . . . Home Planners make every effort to process and ship each order for blueprints and books within 48 hours. Because of this, we have deemed it unnecessary to acknowledge receipt of our customers orders. See order coupon for the postage and handling charges for surface mail, air mail or foreign mail.

4. A NOTE REGARDING REVERSE BLUEPRINTS . . . As a special service to those wishing to build in reverse of the plan as shown, we do include an extra set of reversed blueprints for only $30.00 additional with each order. Even though the lettering and dimensions appear backward on reversed blueprints, they make a handy reference because they show the house just as it's being built in reverse from the standard blueprints — thereby helping you visualize the home better.

5. OUR EXCHANGE POLICY . . . Since blueprints are printed up in specific response to your individual order, we cannot honor requests for refunds. However, the first set of blueprints in any order (or the one set in a single set order) for a given design may be exchanged for a set of another design at a fee of $20.00 plus $3.00 for postage and handling via surface mail; $4.00 via air mail.

TO: HOME PLANNERS, INC., 23761 RESEARCH DRIVE
FARMINGTON HILLS, MICHIGAN 48024

Please rush me the following:

_____ SET(S) BLUEPRINTS FOR DESIGN NO(S). _____ $_____
Single Set, $125.00; Additional Identical Sets in Same Order $30.00 ea.
4 Set Package of Same Design, $175.00 (Save $40.00) 8 Set Package of Same Design, $225.00 (Save ($110.00) 1 Specification Outline included.

_____ MATERIALS LIST Just $25.00 for Entire Order (1 List per Set) . . . . $_____

_____ SPECIFICATION OUTLINES @ $3.00 EACH . . . . $_____

_____ DETAIL SETS @ $12.95 ea. or both @ $19.95: ☐ PLUMBING ☐ELECTRICAL $_____

Michigan Residents add 4% sales tax $_____

FOR POSTAGE ☐ $3.00 Added to Order for Surface Mail (UPS) – Any Mdse.
AND HANDLING ☐ $4.00 Added for Priority Mail of One-Three Sets of Blueprints.
PLEASE CHECK ☐ $6.00 Added for Priority Mail of Four or more Sets of Blueprints. } $_____
✓ & REMIT ☐ For Canadian orders add $2.00 to above applicable rates

☐ C.O.D. PAY POSTMAN
(C.O.D. Within U.S.A. Only) TOTAL in U.S.A. funds $_____

PLEASE PRINT
Name _____
Street _____
City _____ State _____ Zip _____

CREDIT CARD ORDERS ONLY: Fill in the boxes below Prices subject to change without notice
Credit Card No. [ ][ ][ ][ ][ ][ ][ ][ ][ ][ ][ ][ ][ ][ ][ ] Expiration Date Month/Year [ ][ ][ ][ ]

CHECK ONE: ☐ **VISA** ☐ **MasterCard**
Order Form Key BK118 Your Signature _____

BLUEPRINT ORDERS SHIPPED WITHIN 48 HOURS OF RECEIPT!

TO: HOME PLANNERS, INC., 23761 RESEARCH DRIVE
FARMINGTON HILLS, MICHIGAN 48024

Please rush me the following:

_____ SET(S) BLUEPRINTS FOR DESIGN NO(S). _____ $_____
Single Set, $125.00; Additional Identical Sets in Same Order $30.00 ea.
4 Set Package of Same Design, $175.00 (Save $40.00) 8 Set Package of Same Design, $225.00 (Save $110.00) 1 Specification Outline included.

_____ MATERIALS LIST Just $25.00 for Entire Order (1 List per Set) . . . . $_____

_____ SPECIFICATION OUTLINES @ $3.00 EACH . . . . $_____

_____ DETAIL SETS @ $12.95 ea. or both @ $19.95: ☐ PLUMBING ☐ELECTRICAL $_____

Michigan Residents add 4% sales tax $_____

FOR POSTAGE ☐ $3.00 Added to Order for Surface Mail (UPS) – Any Mdse.
AND HANDLING ☐ $4.00 Added for Priority Mail of One-Three Sets of Blueprints.
PLEASE CHECK ☐ $6.00 Added for Priority Mail of Four or more Sets of Blueprints. } $_____
✓ & REMIT ☐ For Canadian orders add $2.00 to above applicable rates

☐ C.O.D. PAY POSTMAN
(C.O.D. Within U.S.A. Only) TOTAL in U.S.A. funds $_____

PLEASE PRINT
Name _____
Street _____
City _____ State _____ Zip _____

CREDIT CARD ORDERS ONLY: Fill in the boxes below Prices subject to change without notice
Credit Card No. [ ][ ][ ][ ][ ][ ][ ][ ][ ][ ][ ][ ][ ][ ][ ] Expiration Date Month/Year [ ][ ][ ][ ]

CHECK ONE: ☐ **VISA** ☐ **MasterCard**
Order Form Key BK118 Your Signature _____

How many sets of blueprints should be ordered?

This question is often asked. The answer can range anywhere from 1 to 8 sets, depending upon circumstances. For instance, a single set of blueprints of your favorite design is sufficient to study the house in greater detail. On the other hand, if you are planning to get cost estimates, or if you are planning to build, you may need as many as eight sets of blueprints. Because the first set of blueprints in each order is $125.00, and because additional sets of the same design in each order are only $30.00 each (and with package sets even more economical), you save considerably by ordering your total requirements now. To help you determine the exact number of sets please refer to the handy check list.

How Many Blueprints Do You Need?

___OWNER'S SET(S)

___**BUILDER** (Usually requires at least 3 sets: 1 as legal document; 1 for inspection; and at least 1 for tradesmen — usually more.)

___**BUILDING PERMIT** (Sometimes 2 sets are required.)

___**MORTGAGE SOURCE** (Usually 1 set for a conventional mortgage; 3 sets for F.H.A. or V.A. type mortgages.)

___**SUBDIVISION COMMITTEE** (If any.)

___**TOTAL NO. SETS REQUIRED**

Blueprint Ordering Hotline–

Phone toll free: 1-800-521-6797.
Orders received by 11 a.m. (Detroit time) will be processed the same day and shipped to you the following day. Use of this line restricted to blueprint ordering only. Michigan residents simply call collect 0-313-477-1850.

Kindly Note: When ordering by phone, please state Order Form Key No. located in box at lower left corner of blueprint order form.

In Canada Mail To:
Home Planners, Inc., 20 Cedar St. North
Kitchener, Ontario N2H 2W8
Phone: (519) 743-4169

Heritage Houses

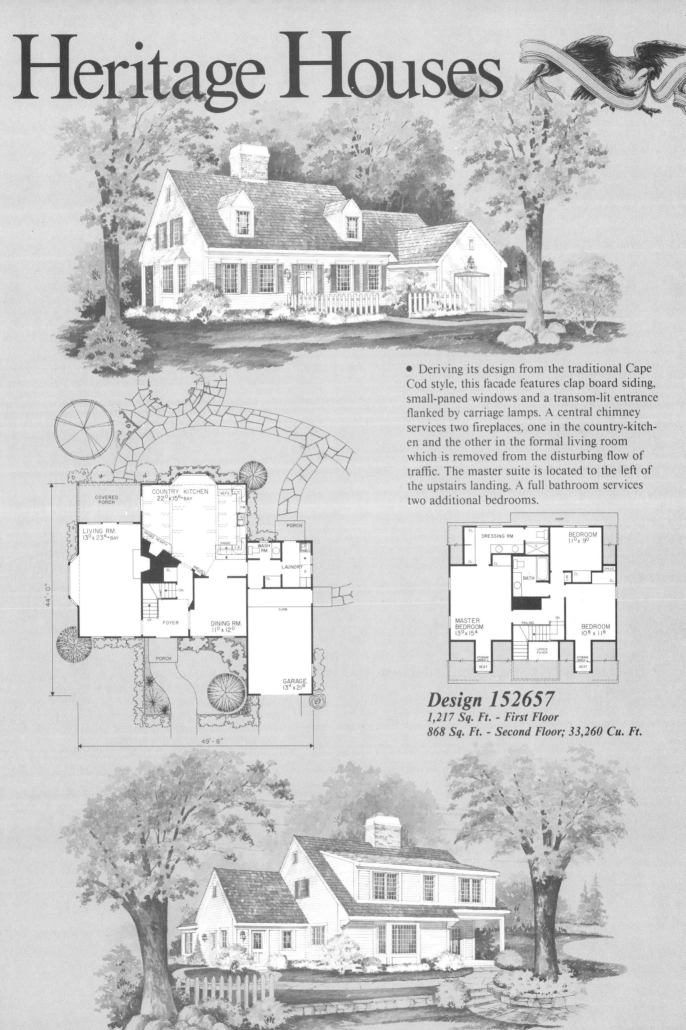

• Deriving its design from the traditional Cape Cod style, this facade features clap board siding, small-paned windows and a transom-lit entrance flanked by carriage lamps. A central chimney services two fireplaces, one in the country-kitchen and the other in the formal living room which is removed from the disturbing flow of traffic. The master suite is located to the left of the upstairs landing. A full bathroom services two additional bedrooms.

Design 152657

1,217 Sq. Ft. - First Floor
868 Sq. Ft. - Second Floor; 33,260 Cu. Ft.

Design 152658
1,218 Sq. Ft. - First Floor
764 Sq. Ft. - Second Floor; 29,690 Cu. Ft.

• Traditional charm of yesteryear is exemplified delightfully in this one-and-a-half story home. The garage has been conveniently tucked away in the rear of the house which makes this design ideal for a corner lot. Interior livability has been planned for efficient living. The front living room is large and features a fireplace with wood box. The laundry area is accessible by way of both the garage and a side covered porch. Enter the rear terrace from both eating areas, the formal dining room and the informal breakfast room.

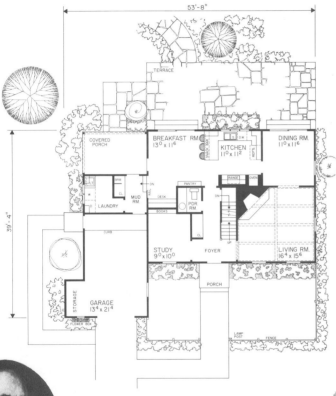

Design 152656 *1,122 Sq. Ft. - First Floor*
884 Sq. Ft. - Second Floor; 31,845 Cu. Ft.

• This charming Cape cottage possesses a great sense of shelter through its gambrel roof. Dormers at front and rear pierce the gambrel roof to provide generous, well-lit living space on the second floor which houses three bedrooms. This design's first floor layout is not far different from that of the Cape cottages of the 18th century. The large kitchen and adjoining dining room recall cottage keeping rooms, in function and location at the rear of the house.

Design 152661
1,020 Sq. Ft. - First Floor
777 Sq. Ft. - Second Floor; 30,745 Cu. Ft.

● Any other starter house or retirement home couldn't have more charm than this design. Its compact frame houses a very livable plan. An outstanding feature of the first floor is the large country kitchen. Its fine attractions include a beamed ceiling, raised hearth fireplace, built-in window seat and a door leading to the outdoors. A living room is in the front of the plan and has another fireplace which shares the single chimney. The rear dormered second floor houses the sleeping and bath facilities.

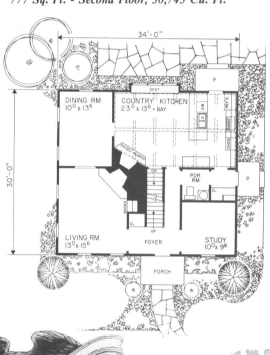

Design 152655
893 Sq. Ft. - First Floor
652 Sq. Ft. - Second Floor; 22,555 Cu. Ft.

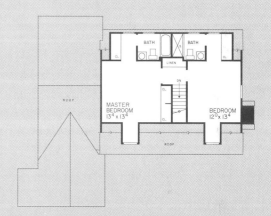

● Wonderful things can be enclosed in small packages. This is the case for this one-and-a-half story design. The total square footage is a mere 1,545 square feet yet its features are many, indeed. Its exterior appeal is very eye-pleasing with horizontal lines and two second story dormers. Livability will be enjoyed in this plan. The front study is ideal for a quiet escape. Nearby is a powder room also convenient to the kitchen and breakfast room. Two bedrooms and two full baths are located on the second floor.

Design 152615 *2,563 Sq. Ft. - First Floor; 552 Sq. Ft. - Second Floor; 59,513 Cu. Ft.*

● The exterior detailing of this design recalls 18th-Century New England architecture. The narrow clapboards and shuttered, multi-paned windows help its detail. Arched entry ways forming covered porches lead to the master bedroom and the other to the service entrance. Enter by way of the centered front door and you are greeted into the foyer. Directly to the right is the study or optional bedroom or to the left is the living room. This large formal room features a fireplace and sliding glass doors to the sun-drenched solarium. The beauty of the solarium will be appreciated from two other rooms besides the living room; the master bedroom and the dining room. All of these rooms have sliding glass doors for easy access. The work center will function efficiently. When it comes time for informal living, this design's family room is outstanding. Beamed ceiling and fireplace are only two of its many features. Other notable features include two sets of multi-paned sliding glass doors which lead to the rear terrace, a built-in wet bar which has room for bar stools, a large built-in desk and easy access to the service area housing the laundry facilities. In addition to the first floor master bedroom, there are two bedrooms and a bath upstairs. The detailing that this design offers will be appreciated for a lifetime by every member of the family.

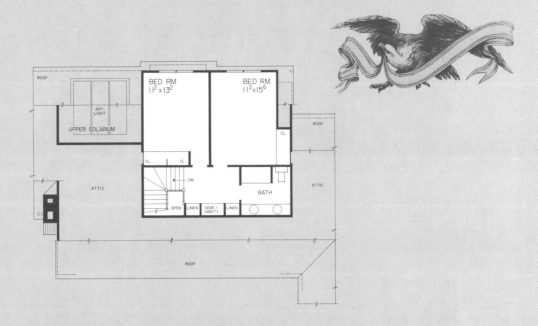

New England Cape Cod Lets The Sun In

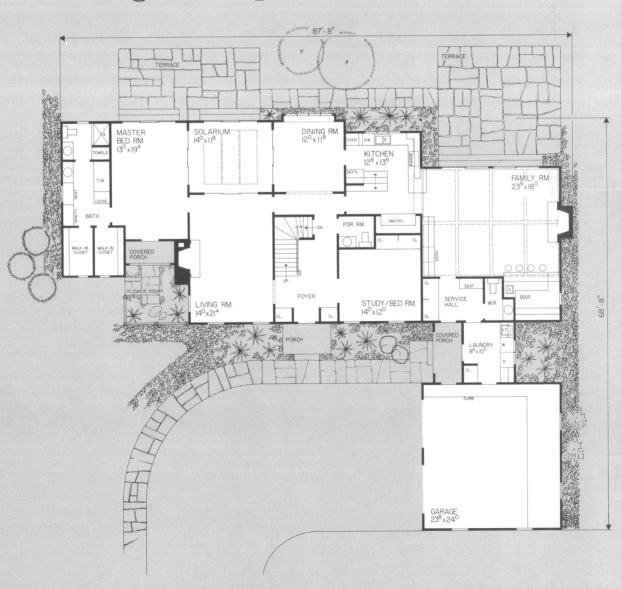

Upper floor plan:

- BED RM. $11^2 \times 13^2$
- BED RM. $11^2 \times 15^6$
- UPPER SOLARIUM
- SKY LIGHT
- ROOF
- ATTIC
- CL.
- DN
- OPEN
- LINEN
- DESK / VANITY
- LINEN
- BATH
- CL.

Main floor plan:

- 87'-8"
- 68'-8"
- TERRACE
- TERRACE
- MASTER BED RM. $13^0 \times 19^4$
- SOLARIUM $14^0 \times 11^8$
- DINING RM. $12^0 \times 11^8$
- KITCHEN $12^8 \times 13^6$
- FAMILY RM. $23^8 \times 18^0$
- TOWELS
- TUB
- LEDGE
- SEAT
- VANITY
- BATH
- OVEN
- D.W.
- REF'G
- RANGE
- WALK-IN CLOSET
- WALK-IN CLOSET
- COVERED PORCH
- PDR. RM.
- PANTRY
- CL.
- CL.
- DESK
- FLOWER COURT
- LIVING RM. $14^0 \times 21^4$
- UP
- DN.
- FOYER
- STUDY/BED RM. $14^0 \times 12^0$
- SERVICE HALL
- SEAT
- BAR
- W.R.
- S
- CL.
- PORCH
- COVERED PORCH
- LAUNDRY $8^8 \times 10^0$
- W.
- D.
- CL.
- CURB
- GARAGE $23^8 \times 24^0$

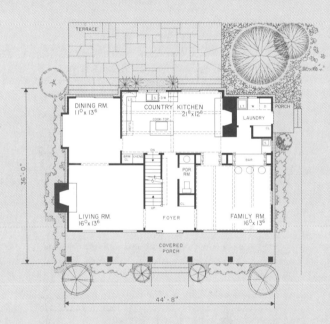

• The exterior of this full two-story is highlighted by the covered porch and balcony. Many enjoyable hours will be spent at these outdoor areas. The interior is highlighted by a spacious country kitchen. Be sure to notice its island cook-top, fireplace and the beamed ceiling. A built-in bar is in the family room.

Design 152664
1,308 Sq. Ft. - First Floor
1,262 Sq. Ft. - Second Floor; 49,215 Cu. Ft.

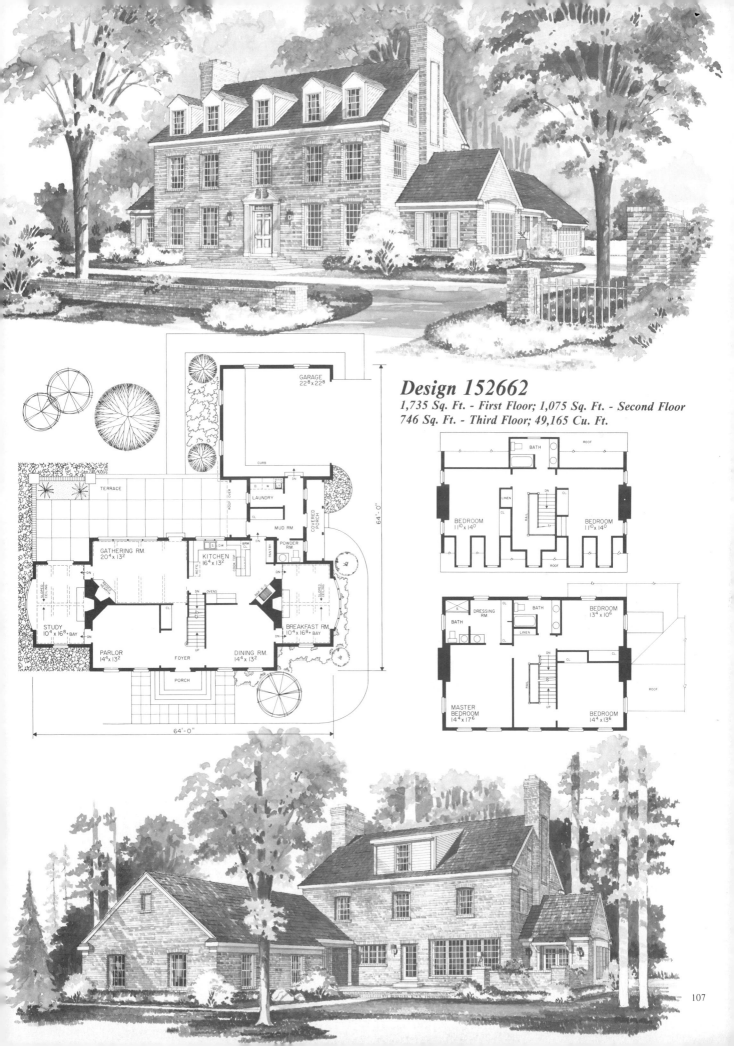

Design 152662

1,735 Sq. Ft. - First Floor; 1,075 Sq. Ft. - Second Floor
746 Sq. Ft. - Third Floor; 49,165 Cu. Ft.

GARAGE
22⁸ x 22⁸

LAUNDRY

MUD RM.

CL

TERRACE

GATHERING RM.
20⁴ x 13²

KITCHEN
16⁴ x 13²

POWDER RM.

PANTRY

COVERED PORCH

STUDY
10⁴ x 16⁸ + BAY

OVENS

BREAKFAST RM.
10⁴ x 16⁸ + BAY

PARLOR
14⁴ x 13²

FOYER

DINING RM.
14⁴ x 13²

PORCH

64'-0"

64'-0"

BATH

ROOF

LINEN

CL

DN

CL

HALL

BEDROOM
11¹⁰ x 14⁰

BEDROOM
11¹⁰ x 14⁰

ROOF

BATH

DRESSING RM.

BATH

LINEN

BEDROOM
13⁴ x 10⁶

HALL

DN

CL

CL

ROOF

MASTER BEDROOM
14⁴ x 17⁶

UP

BEDROOM
14⁴ x 13⁶

A Charleston Single House

Design 152660

1,479 Sq. Ft. - First Floor
1,501 Sq. Ft. - Second Floor
912 Sq. Ft. - Third Floor
556 Sq. Ft. - Activities Room Area
57,440 Cu. Ft.

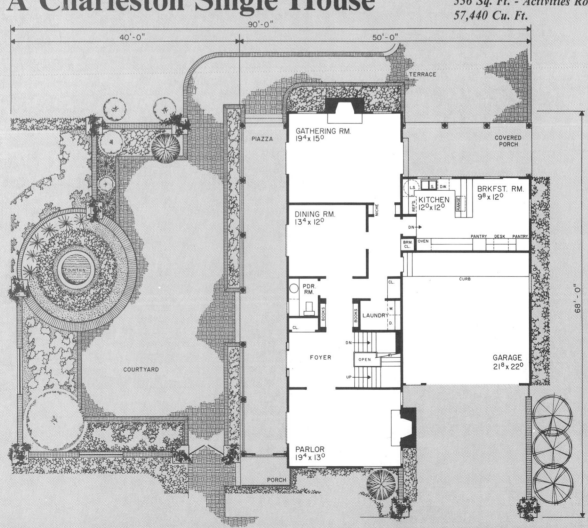

90'-0"

40'-0" 50'-0"

68'-0"

TERRACE

GATHERING RM.
19⁴ x 15⁰

PIAZZA

COVERED PORCH

KITCHEN
12⁰ x 12⁰

BRKFST. RM.
9⁸ x 12⁰

DINING RM.
13⁴ x 12⁰

NICHE

REFS. RANGE

DN.

OVEN PANTRY DESK PANTRY

BRM
CL.

CURB

PDR.
RM.

BOOKS

CL.

LAUNDRY
W.
D.

BOOKS

FOUNTAIN

CL.

DN.

FOYER

OPEN

UP

COURTYARD

GARAGE
21⁸ x 22⁰

PARLOR
19⁴ x 13⁰

PORCH

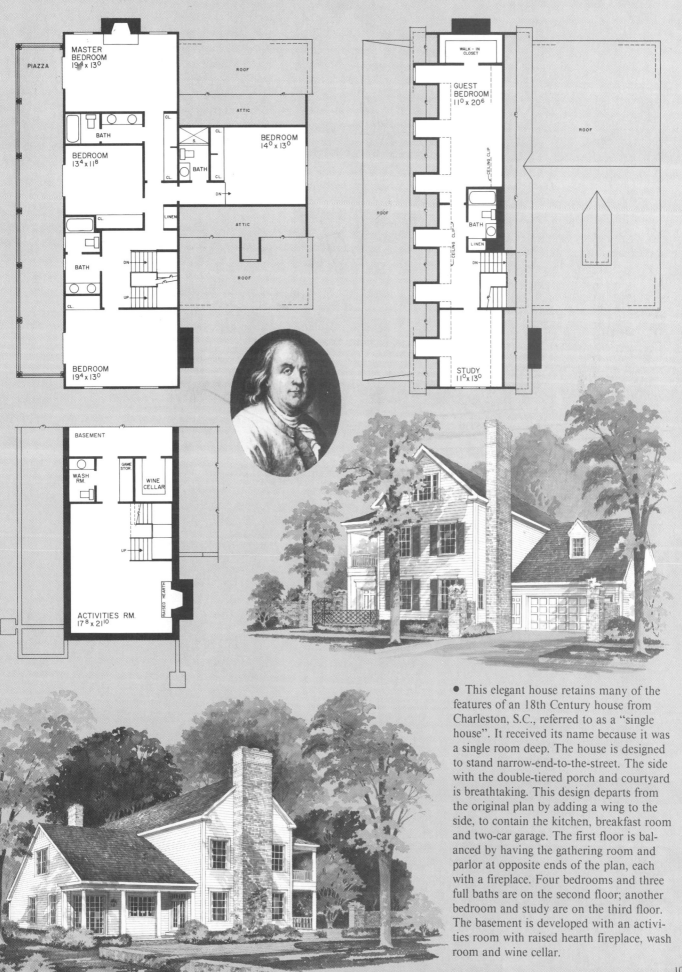

MASTER BEDROOM 19⁴ x 13⁰

PIAZZA

BATH

BEDROOM 13⁴ x 11⁸

CL.

BATH

CL.

S.

BATH

CL.

CL.

BEDROOM 14⁰ x 13⁰

LINEN

ATTIC

ATTIC

ROOF

ROOF

DN

BATH

CL.

DN

UP

BEDROOM 19⁴ x 13⁰

WALK - IN CLOSET

GUEST BEDROOM 11⁰ x 20⁶

ROOF

ROOF

CEILING CLIP

CEILING CLIP

BATH

LINEN

DN

STUDY 11⁰ x 13⁰

BASEMENT

WASH RM.

GAME STOR.

WINE CELLAR

UP

RAISED HEARTH

ACTIVITIES RM. 17⁸ x 21¹⁰

• This elegant house retains many of the features of an 18th Century house from Charleston, S.C., referred to as a "single house". It received its name because it was a single room deep. The house is designed to stand narrow-end-to-the-street. The side with the double-tiered porch and courtyard is breathtaking. This design departs from the original plan by adding a wing to the side, to contain the kitchen, breakfast room and two-car garage. The first floor is balanced by having the gathering room and parlor at opposite ends of the plan, each with a fireplace. Four bedrooms and three full baths are on the second floor; another bedroom and study are on the third floor. The basement is developed with an activities room with raised hearth fireplace, wash room and wine cellar.

Design 152650
1,451 Sq. Ft. - First Floor
1,091 Sq. Ft. - Second Floor; 43,555 Cu. Ft.

● The rear view of this design is just as appealing as the front. The dormers and the covered porch with pillars is a charming way to introduce this house to the on-lookers. Inside, the appeal is also outstanding. Note the size (18 x 25) of the gathering room which is open to the dining room. Kitchen-nook area is very spacious and features an island range, built-in desk and more. It is a great convenience having the laundry in the service area which is close to the kitchen. Imagine, a fireplace in both the gathering room and the master bedroom! Make special note of the front and rear service entrances.

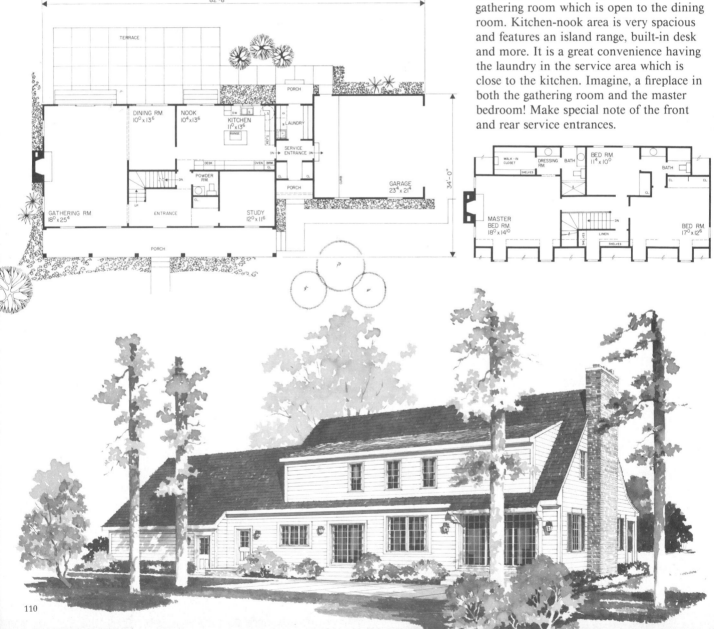

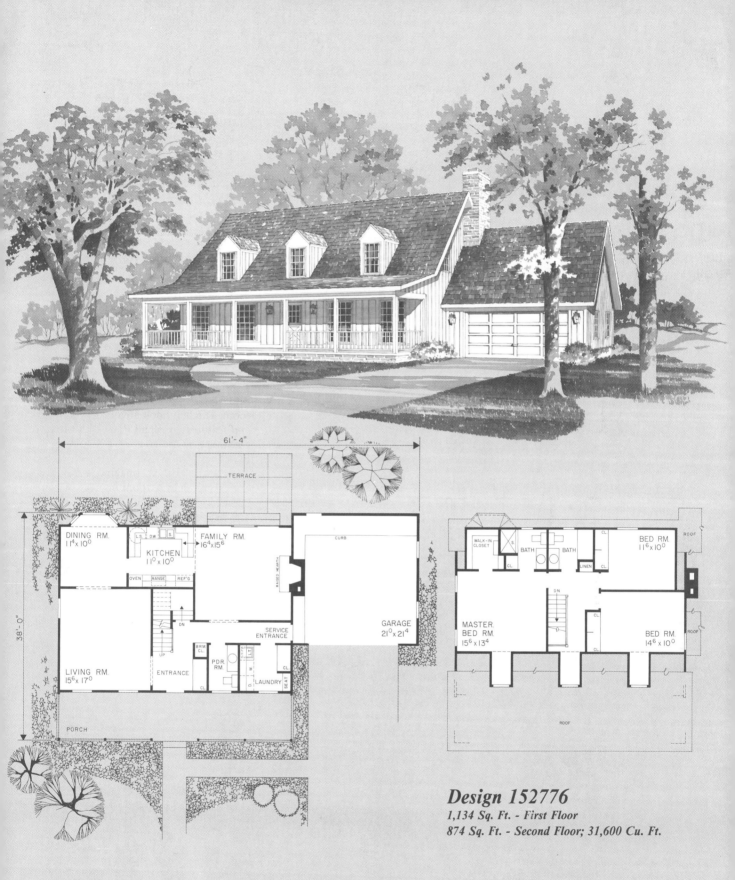

Design 152776
1,134 Sq. Ft. - First Floor
874 Sq. Ft. - Second Floor; 31,600 Cu. Ft.

● This board-and-batten farmhouse design has all of the country charm of New England. The large front covered porch surely will be appreciated during the beautiful warm weather months. Immediately off the front entrance is the delightful corner living room. The dining room with bay window will be easily served by the U-shaped kitchen. Informal family living enjoyment will be obtained in the family room which features a raised hearth fireplace, sliding glass doors to the rear terrace and easy access to the work center of powder room, laundry and service entrance. The second floor houses all of the sleeping facilities. There is a master bedroom with a private bath and walk-in closet. Two other bedrooms share a bath. This is an excellent one-and-a-half story design.

Design 152644

1,349 Sq. Ft. - First Floor
836 Sq. Ft. - Second Floor
36,510 Cu. Ft.

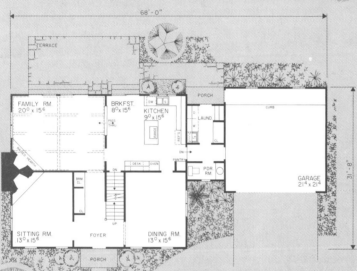

● What a delightful, compact two-story this is! This design has many fine features tucked within its framework. The bowed roofline of this house stems from late 17th-Century architecture.